table inspirations

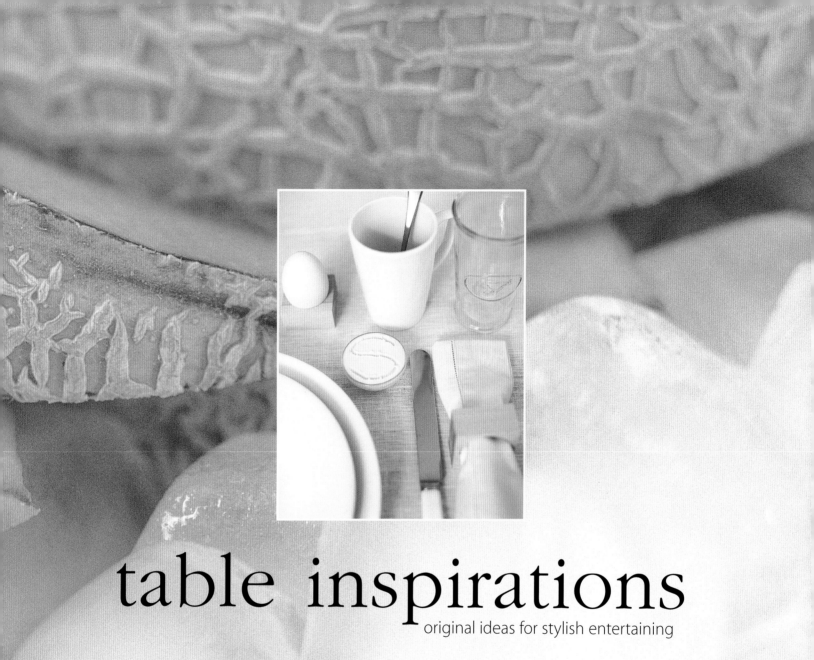

table inspirations

original ideas for stylish entertaining

RYLAND
PETERS
& SMALL
London New York

emily chalmers

photography by david brittain

Designer Catherine Randy
Senior editor Sophie Bevan
Location research Emily Chalmers, Kate Brunt,
                       Sarah Hepworth
Production Patricia Harrington
Art director Gabriella Le Grazie
Publishing director Alison Starling

Stylist Emily Chalmers

First published in the United Kingdom in 2001
by Ryland Peters & Small
20–21 Jockey's Fields
London WC1R 4BW
www.rylandpeters.com

This paperback edition first published in 2005

ISBN 1 84172 917 5

A CIP record for this book is available from
the British Library

Printed in China

contents

introduction

Whatever the occasion – be it festive or everyday, grand or intimate – it's easy to create an atmosphere that will make your guests feel relaxed, happy and welcome at the table.

Whether is it a birthday buffet for ten guests, a family group of six sitting down for Christmas dinner, or an intimate table for two to celebrate an anniversary – setting a table is all about entertaining your guests. What makes the occasion special is the choice, the combination and the positioning of china, glassware, flowers, candles and linen.

When buying flowers, carefully consider the shapes and colours that would best decorate the table and surrounding area. Pop namecards at each setting to make the guests feel special – when you are pushed for time, these need only be squares of card dropped into empty drinking glasses or wedged under a little pebble at the edge of each plate. And there are plenty of ways that linen and cutlery can be attractively displayed – fold the napkin around the cutlery and tie with ribbon, or place a folded napkin flat under each dinner plate with cutlery sitting to one side.

The aim of this book is to illustrate that it is the little details that make all the difference. Modern mealtimes tend to be informal, so there is no need to feel confined by the old 'rules' – a table can still look 'smart' without sticking to a more conventional setting, so long as it remains well considered and orderly. The examples given in this book are here to inspire and excite – mix them with your own ideas and, most of all, have fun!

above and right Practical ideas are often the best: an old glass brick makes an interesting holder for a basic church candle, and frozen slices of lime are a colourful and cooling ingredient for a refreshing summer drink.
opposite Simple and orderly, while still being decorative, this table setting is ideal for a casual meal with friends.

The elements are the basic ingredients of every table setting – these include linen, cutlery, china, glassware, flowers, namecards and lighting. This section of the book explores different ways of using these components to create the look you desire for your table. It is the choice and presentation of the table elements that make a setting unique to a particular meal. For example, personalized place settings will make guests feel special; carefully selected blooms will emphasize a colour scheme, and the textures of the table linen or subtle changes to the lighting can add drama and atmosphere to the occasion.

the elements

Cups, plates and bowls are perhaps the most obvious elements of a table setting. There are many styles, colours and textures to choose from, so play around with different combinations.

cups, plates and bowls

The cups, plates and bowls you choose depend very much on the food and drinks you are serving and the style of the meal. Some occasions call for a large pasta dish, others warrant dinner plate, side plate and soup bowl – and there are many options for occasions that require no china settings at all.

Good, basic white utility china is indispensable. Plates can be used to eat off, to serve from or as 'mats' for other pieces. Bowls are good for soup, pasta and salad, as well as for dessert. And cups or beakers can be used for drinks, desserts and flowers. The variations are almost endless.

Pretty dainty china is also fun to own – try mixing and matching old teacups and saucers for a traditional English tea. Use a special teacup for sugar cubes and a floral milk jug to display flowers.

Serving bowls always come in handy, and you can never have too many. They are excellent for a formal meal, but can also be used with floating candles or flower heads for a more relaxed

above It's great to have tall stacks of everyday china to choose from. Invest in a plain white, good-quality service and gradually add other colours and styles that take your fancy.
right A beautifully proportioned teacup needn't be used only for drinking tea – it makes an excellent home for a pretty flower head, too! Lay it on top of a stack of plain china for an interesting display. It can be put to one side once the meal has commenced.

left There's no need to stick to matching sets of china. Soft pastel colours look good all mixed together. Use a soft-green cup on a baby-blue saucer and stack them on top of white or pale-pink plates and bowls.

below This simple ceramic version of a coffee filter makes a stylish addition to a breakfast-table setting. Look out for individual teapots and juicers, too, so your guests to help themselves.

left A simple small bowl placed on top of a neutral napkin is used here to make an individual place setting. Nutmegs, small washed pebbles or single flower heads can be added to give a personal touch. The combination of linen, ceramic and metal used here on a dark, thick wooden table top is striking, and the overall look is softened with bright flowers.
above Choose organically shaped dishes made from natural materials. You can never have enough tiny platters to hold olives, rock salt, roughly ground black pepper, and a selection of nuts and seeds to nibble on with pre-dinner drinks.

Make the most of your table elements: keep glassware clean and bright; carefully stack china at a setting; and choose vessels that are dual purpose to display and serve food and drink.

this page, main Simple clear glass bowls are an invaluable element of a practical kitchen. Use these to mix in, bake in and serve from.
below right The floral decoration on this elegant china helps to soften the otherwise cold look of the setting, and stacking all three pieces creates interesting layers.

occasion. Stemmed bowls and dishes are great for displaying fruit, but will look equally good at a Christmas table, full of colourful baubles. Or why not mix the fruit with the baubles?

Keep a look out for china versions of other tableware – ceramic coffee filters are practical and stylish, and often less expensive than electrical gadgets or large glass cafetières. You can also get ceramic fruit juicers that will look good at a breakfast table.

If a certain piece of china catches your eye, don't worry about having to buy a 'set'; keep it as a special individual item that can

be mixed with other pieces or used on its own. If in doubt, try to stick to mixing either colour or pattern, so the table never looks too cluttered. Pairs of china can be used effectively, too, such as bowls to hold floating candles or dishes to offer rock salt and coarsely ground black pepper.

Look out for one-off pieces – it may be an interesting decorative dish that you have picked up on your travels, or an old silver tray handed down in the family. The dish could be perfect holding a large pillar candle surrounded by pebbles as a centrepiece to a table; the tray might be great for a birthday buffet, piled with olives sitting on a bed of large green leaves.

The main rule with china is to play around and go with what looks right. If you don't have enough pieces to lay formal settings for everyone, then mix and match different sets or use wooden bowls and napkins for salad, bread and other extras – there is no rule that you have to eat from china plates and drink from china cups! Wooden platters, tin pots, glass bowls – this is where it is easy to add character and express individuality within the table setting. Look out for different materials – these could be your inspiration for a special occasion. Glass plates are an inexpensive way to 'pad out' a dinner service and sit well between pieces of china. Remember

below left **Build up textures:** start with a roughly woven table runner or placemat and juxtapose this against plain linen napkins and soft cool soapstone dishes. Food elements such as nuts, raisins or dried fruit make a stylish table snack and add to the mix of surface textures.

below A lacquer tray provides a good base for a modern layered setting. Glass plates enable colours to show up and enhance the look. Tiny individual bottles of drink and foil-wrapped biscuits and sweets give a quirky touch.

that special large plates, dishes and trays can always be used as lay plates – these are not for eating from, but rather act to define individual settings and make an interesting first layer at each place.

Use large shells to hold nuts, or papier-mâché bowls for bread. A marble bowl could house a single floating gloriosa head or some sliced exotic fruit – use your imagination!

Mix and match different materials for drinking vessels, too. Red wine and coloured fruit juices look great in silver or pewter beakers and goblets. And their reflective surfaces will create interesting effects around the table. Ceramic beakers will also work well if they are in keeping with the rest of the tableware.

Mix materials – ceramic, wood, glass, tin, stone – and lay them over different textures, such as lacquer, cloth and woven matting.

glasses and decanters

Clean, bright glassware adds a sparkling touch to
any table setting. Collect whatever takes your
fancy and enjoy mixing and matching.

Glasses, bottles, jugs and decanters are very versatile
table elements. As well as being used for drinks,
interesting pieces can be used to display flowers and
hold tealights and floating candles. Cut, coloured,
recycled, thick, dainty – there are so many styles and
varieties available, but the most important thing is to
make sure all your glassware is as clean and shiny as
possible. Remove stubborn water stains by soaking
in vinegar, and change flower water regularly.

Scour second-hand shops and antique markets
for one-off pieces of coloured cut glass – these might
just give that extra-special touch that your table top
needs. If any of these favourite pieces get chipped,
there's no need to throw them away. Simply file
away any dangerous surfaces and reuse them to hold
candles and tealights or sweets and sugar cubes.

Plain pieces of drinking glassware can be jazzed
up with temporary stick-on decorations or tattoos, or

opposite left Tiny pieces of edible flower petals have been set in ice for a pretty summer drink.

opposite right These tall glasses have been rubbed with lemon juice and dipped in a bowl of decorative sugar to give them a special crystallized rim.

below This green beaker picks out the colours of the flowers and candles. A big glass jar provides a good container for pastel-coloured bonbons.

right These plain heavy-duty beakers have been given a special touch with the addition of simple stick-on bindis – readily available from Indian shops and markets.

Plain, recycled, etched, coloured, cut ... mix pieces together
for a timeless and eclectic look on your table top.

use jewellery wire to attach sequins, tiny gems or small buttons around plain water tumblers. Flat jewel-like decorations and glitter confetti can also be stuck onto glassware with non-toxic adhesive. There are lots of different etching and transfer kits that you can have fun with, too.

Don't be afraid to mix old and new pieces of glassware, and different colours and shapes can also look very effective side by side on the table. Choose the odd piece in a complementary colour to dot around a table and enhance a particular scheme.

Because of the transparent quality of most table glassware, it is the element that can be most easily dressed up or down to complement the mood of a particular occasion. Make the most of this feature – fill bottles with coloured water purely for decoration. Use large clear-glass tumblers to present interesting and exotic fruit salads, and so on. Think how different you can make a table top appear by substituting cut glass with smooth plain glass pieces, or by filling tumblers with cranberry juice rather than water at each place setting. A few candles placed in

above left Scour antique shops and markets for special pieces. This old jug would never be strong enough to carry liquids but makes a dainty holder for sugar stirrers.
above These basic handmade tumblers are ideal for serving juice or yoghurt at the breakfast table.

left Collect interesting pieces of glassware to mix and match on your table top. Special wineglasses can also be used for fruit juice or sparkling water and need not be kept back purely for elegant dining.

above If you are not fortunate enough to have your milk delivered in traditional glass bottles, secure one and reuse it in place of a jug on the table top. Little glass mugs and cups make interesting beakers for cold drinks.

Choose clear tall glasses to show off bright cocktails and use simple glass votives to serve rows of vodka jellies. Perfect for a party setting!

antique coloured cut-glass wineglasses will add a very decadent quality to an otherwise plain spread.

Collect one-off decanters to add a twist to the table top – red wine not only tastes better when presented in a decanter, but looks better, too. Introduce decanters for any colourful drinks you are serving – diluted lime-juice cordial and fruit juices. Decanters can also be used for table-top flowers; even a narrow-necked vessel will hold a couple of beautiful stems of orchids and look elegant on your table. If you want to get really creative or exploit a dramatic colour scheme, fill your decanters with diluted food colouring and add coordinating flowers for a really vibrant and fun display – perfect for a party or occasion such as New Year's Eve.

The key is to experiment and think laterally – old milk bottles make great vases and are even good as decanters at the right setting. Likewise, an interesting vase might be a good substitute for a decanter – so long as it pours well! Tealight holders can double up as little drinking tumblers, just as interesting drinking glasses can be used to hold candles. Try placing a glass plate on top of a glass vase to create a stemmed dish for a centrepiece – just play around!

above Place knives and forks in interesting envelopes for guests to pick out from a large jar or a decorative galvanized bucket.

right For an informal setting, group pieces of cutlery together in clear utility glass jars – ideal for a large breakfast or brunch, when guests can help themselves according to what they choose to eat.

opposite left Mixing and matching older styles of cutlery can be very effective. For example, varied styles of antique silver cutlery are perfect for classic occasions like a Christmas tea party or a Mother's Day lunch.

opposite below right Plain knives and forks are brought to life with special decorative touches for a buffet-style party.

cutlery

There are many elegant styles of cutlery available, but you can create just as great an impact by stylish presentation of the humblest pieces.

The presentation of cutlery is a useful way to add to the decoration of your table without investing in expensive silver canteens. For a formal sit-down meal, you will probably opt for a traditional setting, such as those shown in the guide to settings (see pages 130–137). However, there are many alternative and elegant ways to lay knives, forks and spoons.

Buffet tables offer great scope: cutlery can be laid out in rows and tied together in a variety of attractive ways. Florists often stock wired decorations, which are perfect for tying individual sets of cutlery. Alternatively, try making your own with a length of wire secured to a flower head or other small decorative object. Make your cutlery festive, too, and decorate a Christmas place setting with a shiny gold bauble tied to the cutlery with rich red ribbon.

napkins and tablecloths

With just a little thought and imagination, napkins, tablecloths and runners can be an easy way to add colour and texture to your setting.

Tablecloths and runners can quickly transform the look of a table and are often a great source of inspiration for the design of the rest of the setting. Apart from being required for practical reasons to protect the table top, they are also an excuse to introduce areas of interesting colour or texture or to dictate the best areas to lay individual settings.

Napkins are relatively inexpensive to buy and it is easy to collect an interesting selection. They are also very simple to make, which means there really are limitless opportunities to be creative with them. If you are making your own table runner or tablecloth from a piece of special fabric, make sure that there is enough spare to make a set of napkins or at least to edge some plain ones to

above left Pick up remnants of satin lining to enhance your table palette. This piece in shocking pink looks great against the shades of green in this layered setting.

above There are many decorative objects that can be used as napkin rings, such as this flower hair band which makes a pretty addition at a tea table. Buy a set in different colours to spread interest around the table – the bands can double as table gifts for your guests to take home after the meal.

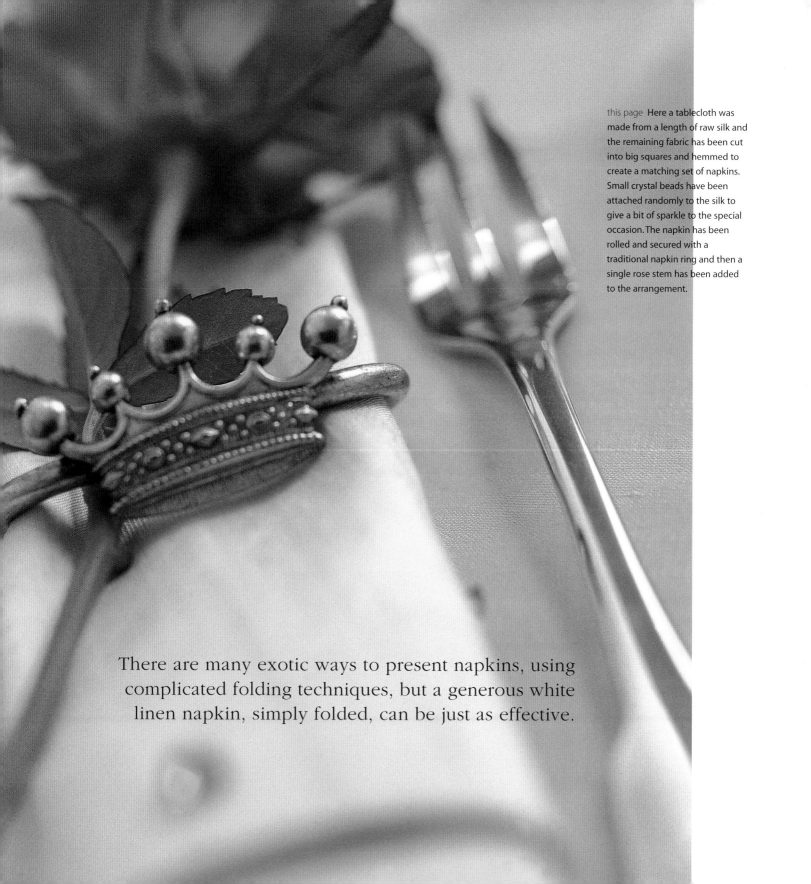

this page Here a tablecloth was made from a length of raw silk and the remaining fabric has been cut into big squares and hemmed to create a matching set of napkins. Small crystal beads have been attached randomly to the silk to give a bit of sparkle to the special occasion. The napkin has been rolled and secured with a traditional napkin ring and then a single rose stem has been added to the arrangement.

There are many exotic ways to present napkins, using complicated folding techniques, but a generous white linen napkin, simply folded, can be just as effective.

below A paper-napkin holder found at a car-boot sale makes an interesting and practical addition to a casual breakfast table top.

right Shades of orange and yellow will brighten up a setting. Choose table linen to coordinate with your china, food or the general dining-room decor, mixing up different textures on the table.

far right An oriental-style table setting has been given colour and texture with satin table linen.

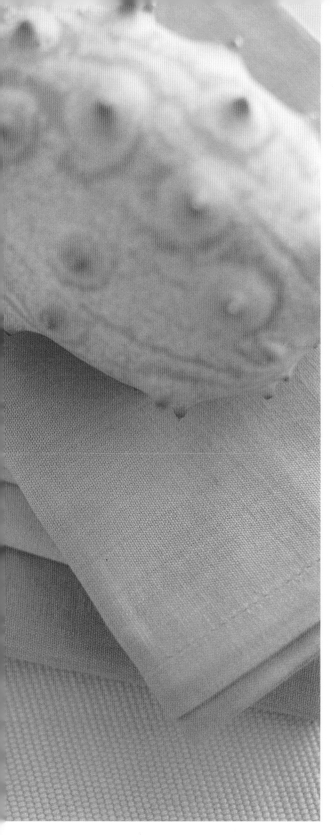

match. Whether you are buying or making napkins, the only criterion should be that you can easily wash them (apart from paper napkins, of course!).

The way you display napkins on the table can be as important as the napkins themselves, and will add character to your special occasion. We have all seen intricately folded napkins – making shapes, such as swans, mitres, peacock tails – this can be interesting. But you needn't be skilled in the art of origami in order to present a napkin effectively. While, traditionally, the napkin is positioned on the left of the setting, it is fun to think of new and interesting alternatives. Sometimes a dinner plate will sit well on a napkin folded lengthways. Sometimes the napkin acts as a good divider between two pieces of china and, if you choose your colours carefully, you can create some interesting layers by laying the napkin in a stack of plates and bowls at each setting. Napkins look good with cutlery, too, especially for a buffet occasion, when they can all be wrapped together with a length of pretty ribbon – or with ivy at Christmas time, for example.

this page Personalizing an boiled egg at a breakfast table will organize your guests and bring a smile to their faces first thing in the morning. This inflatable egg cup is also good at a children's party.

opposite left A piece of birthday cake and little party gifts have been put into these takeaway containers to give away at a children's party. Liquid cake icing has been used to write each guest's name on their individual box, which was then secured with coloured string and tied to a balloon.

opposite right These little acrylic cubes are ideal for holding namecards to sit neatly at each place setting.

namecards

There are numerous ways to create personalized place settings, and the more inspirational you are, the more special your guests will feel when they come to sit down at the table.

When coming up with ideas for namecards, try to incorporate elements from the existing setting, such as using a cocktail stick to flag a card from an empty glass or, for a special breakfast or tea-time treat, carve an initial in an individual butter pat or write a name on a boiled egg.

Alternatively, create special individual arrangements around a handwritten namecard using found objects that reflect the setting of the meal, such as a flower petal to echo the floral theme of the decorations or a pebble from the beach or garden if dining alfresco. Another idea is to write names on old-fashioned luggage or price labels, and then tie them to the handles of cutlery at each setting or to a single decorative bloom. Labelled table gifts are a good way to mark each place, and a personalized label will turn the simplest flower stem laid on each plate or napkin into a special gift for each guest.

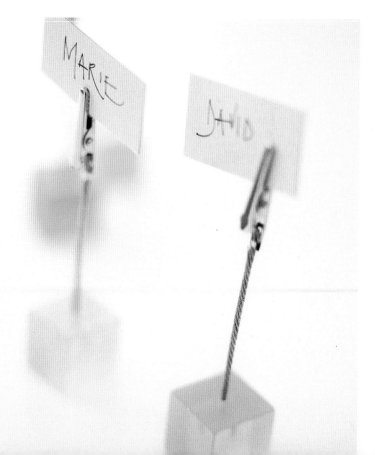

below A planting tag is used at each place setting for this children's party. A miniature cactus has been carefully planted in an acrylic pot as a gift for each child to take home after the event.

right There are many styles of namecard holders in the shops today. This set of tiny handbags is particularly quirky. Write your guests' names in a coloured ink that coordinates with the rest of the setting.

far right A plain brown luggage tag sits happily strung around this denim napkin. Tying the fork into the bundle is ideal for a buffet or barbecue situation.

There are also plenty of namecard holders that can be bought for more formal occasions. Look out for sets that include slightly different pieces along the same theme, so that each guest feels that his or her setting is unique. Or – the simplest option can often look the smartest – drop handwritten cards into empty wineglasses or water tumblers at each place. When writing names on the cards, choose an ink colour that will coordinate with the colour scheme of your occasion, such as metallic gold for a Christmas dinner, or pale pink or blue for a christening or baby shower.

The use of namecards will always bring a slight sense of formality to the overall setting, in the way that you, as the host, are dictating the seating arrangements. But this in itself will add an initial element of surprise as your guests discover who they are sitting next to. Why not play on this idea and get guests to pick namecards from a hat to choose their neighbours at the table?

Personalized settings provide you, as the host, with the opportunity to control seating arrangements that could potentially liven up the meal!

placemats and coasters

As potentially the 'building blocks' of a table setting, placemats and coasters are very important elements, bringing interest to an otherwise plain surface.

From a practical point of view, placemats and coasters protect the table surface from moisture and scratches, and may be required to act as insulation for hot plates and bowls placed on top. They also have a decorative function, providing the opportunity to introduce different colours, textures and materials to your table top.

In addition, placemats help to determine a specific area for a single setting, and they can be important elements within a layering theme at each place. You may want to use a mat as a base colour and build upwards with a pile of china elements, or perhaps you would like to see the interesting textures of a square of felt underneath a large glass dinner plate.

Placemats can be made from a wide variety of materials: fabric, cork and rattan provide interesting textures, as do slate, leather and rubber. Slate mats allow for another level of interest: chalk writes well on slate and could be used to personalize place settings or to label mats carrying condiments or dishes for

above left These heavily textured circular sisal placemats look great at an outdoor setting, particularly with the contrasting smooth surface of this soapstone dish. Extend the theme with sisal baskets to hold cutlery and serve textured rustic bread and smooth nuts and seeds for your guests to nibble on.

above Here, again, we see groups of textures working well together. The loosely woven raffia table runner has a fantastic fringed edge. A small square of linen has been sewn into a coaster.

Accentuate textures and shapes on your table top by choosing placemats and coasters in interesting materials. Use rough sisal, spongy cork, raw linen, uneven slate – and have fun!

this page Coasters can be found in all manner of fabrics. These elegant squares are made from a beaded material that adds a touch of decadence to the setting. They are great for special festive occasions – gold at Christmas or pearl beads for a dainty Mother's Day tea table. It is also fun to play around with unexpected objects – inexpensive squares of cork can be used as placemats and cut down to coaster size, and scraps of old roofing slate look great as a background to a contemporary table setting.

right These placemats and coasters have been made from inexpensive grey felt. The felt was cut into squares with sharp scissors and then the corners were rounded off to give an organic feel to an otherwise austere setting. A hole was cut into each mat as a decorative touch. Fabrics such as this work particularly well on a thick glass table top.

below These brightly coloured rubber placemats look striking at a children's party or fun celebration and make a good base for a layered setting. Mix and match primary colours over the table top for a sunny feel.

guests to help themselves to. A large wooden dish could also be used as a placemat and might be an excellent 'container' for the other elements set down, in a similar way to an individual tray. Some plates are large enough to be used as placemats themselves.

Coasters are like small placemats – again serving for protection and for decoration. If it is necessary to use coasters, then it is worth putting some thought into choosing them. Again, there is an opportunity here to enter into the total theme of the setting with the appropriate colours and textures.

It is often possible to pick up coasters that match bought placemats or napkins, but it is by no means necessary to use a matching set. As with placemats, squares and circles of leather or organic shapes cut from felt can look wonderful on a table top. Or use remnants of favourite fabrics – a spare napkin will usually cut down to a full set of matching coasters. Special ceramic tiles can be bought singly and mixed and matched together to create an interesting set of coasters (add a square of felt to the base of any rough surface). Squares of colourful carpet or rubber or lino flooring (often handed over as sample pieces) are great for placemats and coasters at a children's table. And small circular cosmetic mirrors are ideal for sitting under shot glasses at a party. The possibilities are almost endless!

candles and lighting

Playing around with different lighting solutions is one of the quickest ways to change the mood of your table to suit the occasion.

Pay special attention to the lighting – both natural and artificial – of your dining area. A table set in a large bay window surrounded with sunlight will feel bright and airy, while an abundance of small table-top candles will bring a feeling of festivity and intimacy to the meal.

Candles are an obvious lighting solution at a dining table, but they can be used in many imaginative and unexpected ways. Look for unusual candleholders – you needn't go to any expense, as you probably have suitable bowls and jars around the house which you have never thought of employing for lighting!

Traditional nightlights are an inexpensive and versatile option, and make a welcome addition to the table top. They can be placed by each setting, in

above These nightlight holders fix with suction pads to any flat clean surface. They are particularly effective at a window, reflecting spots of light around the room.

right Tiny candles are effective placed at each individual setting. The candle on the right is made from clear gel that burns in a similar way to wax.

Choose candles and lighting carefully to illuminate your table setting. There are many ways of incorporating these extra elements into your chosen theme, whether for practicality or pure decoration.

this page, main Buy bundles of candles that catch your eye – you can never have too many!

below A storm lantern or hurricane lamp is an excellent way of lighting an outdoor setting. Try collecting brightly coloured flower heads from the garden to drop into the glass jar around the base of the candle. If you don't have a table-top lantern, a large vase or jug could be used for a light – just make sure the candle flame stays well clear of any surfaces.

rows across the table, and scattered on surrounding surfaces, giving spots of light all around the room.

There are many types of candles available, and even more ways of displaying them. Try sticking standard dinner candles or tapers upright in a bowl filled with sand or dishwasher salt. Or a single wide pillar candle surrounded by decorative elements, such as flower heads or pebbles, can be as effective as a cluster of smaller candles.

It is fun, too, to be inventive with electric lighting. Try placing a line of fairy lights lengthways along a party table to add spots of light, or attach an artificial

above These galvanized buckets contain candles scented with citronella – a natural insect repellent – which makes them the obvious choice for a garden or balcony party. Place them around the edges of a balcony to illuminate a barbecue scene.
left These little ceramic beakers make excellent holders for nightlights and look particularly effective placed together in a row along a wooden shelf or mantelpiece. Made from fine china, they give a softer, warmer glow than glassware would.

flower head close to each beam for a colourful, funky setting. Fairy lights also work well in a cluster and could be used hanging from a hook on the wall or placed in a coloured glass or plastic serving bowl for an interesting centrepiece.

If you have both, mix electric lighting with candlelight for your occasion. A string of colourful lights hanging over a doorway, around a window frame, or left in a cluster in the far corner of the room will look particularly effective if they echo the glow of tealights in coloured glass bowls on the table top. The lighting can also be spread out and into the garden if you have your table by a set of French doors or a big window. Even if the weather is bad, lanterns or multicoloured outdoor fairy lights can be grouped outside to give an extended colourful glow. If you want to be really clever, mix electric lighting and candlelight for an unusual

above Tiny tin tealight holders light up a modern table setting. Placed here between the guests' placemats, they create glowing lines across the table. For a more informal setting or an outdoor party, you could use recycled tin cans and punch holes in their sides.
left Candle-making kits are widely available and homemade candles have a charm all of their own. Almost any vessel is suitable for a candle pot – these little oriental cups look sweet with coordinating coloured wax in them.

above Whether indoors or outside, a row of Chinese paper lanterns suspended from coordinating pink ribbon looks festive strung above a buffet table.

right There are plenty of lanterns available to buy, but it is also fun to make your own from recycled jam jars and tin cans. Remove labels from glass jars for a clear glow and punch holes in clean tin cans to see dots of light. Simply wind a piece of wire securely around the top of the jar or tin, make a 'handle' and attach to a branch.

You can never have enough lanterns! If you plan to entertain in the garden, make sure you have a good stock of lighting options that won't blow out at the first sign of a breeze.

Electric lighting can be a fun alternative to candles, and fairy lights aren't just for Christmas! These colourful chilli lights look great hanging behind a warmly coloured Halloween or Thanksgiving table top.

centrepiece – why not wind mini fairy lights in a circle around a bowl of floating candles?

It is important to look after candles, particularly if they are the long-lasting variety, such as larger pillar candles or floor-standing models. For a large candle, try to keep it burning no longer than two hours at the first use – this usually ensures even burning and is good to 'start it off'. Always watch that wicks don't get too long – this will create a tall flame that can blacken any nearby paintwork over time. Trim wicks to roughly six millimetres for best burning potential. And try to keep candles away from draughts: a draught will speed up a candle's burning time and cause irregular burning.

below An interesting arrangement has been made here with a glass bowl containing fairy lights arranged around a glitter ball. This bowl has then been positioned inside another glass dish of coloured water. Dilute food colouring to create a colour that coordinates with the rest of the setting, and take care to keep the electrical cables and bulbs away from the water.

below Dainty single stems have been carefully put together to pick out the pinks and whites in this table setting. Cluster groups of vases of different shapes and sizes for added interest. The butterflies give a special decorative touch.

right Single flower heads can look wonderfully elegant sitting in individual vases – tealight holders will work just as well. Cymbidium orchid flowers are extremely effective for this look.

opposite left A single bright gloriosa lily flower is as effective as a whole bunch. Float the flower head in a green bowl to make the colours really stand out.

opposite right Bright artificial flower heads look great on fake turf for a kitsch display.

flowers and plants

Flowers are an obvious way to spruce up your table top for a mealtime or party. There are so many blooms and types of foliage available to choose from – from exotic and unusual species, such as birds-of-paradise, ginger and anthurium, to more humble, cottage-garden flowers, like lavender and marguerites – it is hard to know where to begin.

If you are working to a budget, you will find there is no need to spend too much money on expensive flowers. A few carnation heads floating in a central bowl of water can look as interesting and attractive as a more extravagant orchid. Or, to make your flowers go a long way, try floating petals in individual glass bowls at each setting – tealight holders or shot glasses make excellent small vases and are ideal for this purpose. Single flower heads will also look good dotted around the table, and cymbidium orchids are perfect for this look. Another inexpensive idea is to stick to using foliage: choose exotic leaves or tie strands of long grass carefully around napkins or beakers.

Choose flowers and plants carefully for the occasion – to enhance the atmosphere and to strengthen or pick out areas of colour in your table setting.

above Think carefully about the vases you choose: here, smooth rounded shapes in matt and shiny finishes contrast with the rough textures and strong lines of the table and runner. The neutral tones offset the single, bright stems of orchids perfectly.

left Single sweet-pea flower heads floating in tiny glass bowls – what could be simpler? These holders can be stacked to create an attractive and highly original decoration for the table.

When buying flowers, remember that a single stem can be as effective and eye-catching as an extravagant mixed bouquet.

Fruit and vegetables can also be usefully employed in place of flowers to bring a slightly different decorative look to an occasion. Alternatively, try using whole plants on the table in place of cut flowers. For instance, orchid plants are more readily available nowadays and can be bought relatively inexpensively and then used again and again. At a more informal setting, place gerbera plants in recycled tin cans for a modern fresh look on the table. And miniature cacti are fun planted singly in jam jars at each place setting for a children's party or unconventional gathering.

Carry floral themes all around the dining area – there's no need to restrict decorations to the table. Gather redundant jugs and vases from the kitchen, plant them up with blooms to match your colour scheme, and spread them around the house, wherever your guests can appreciate them.

Flowers also make wonderful table gifts, so treat your guests with individual mini bouquets at the table. Just three or four simple blooms can be tied with ribbon, labelled with each guest's name, and placed in a spare water beaker at every setting.

left Gather cottage-garden flowers, such as sweet peas, roses and viburnum, in soft, pastel tones. Lay extra beakers, like these pretty Moroccan tea glasses, at each place setting to keep the flowers fresh, ready to take home after the meal.

below Here, the dining-room windowsill is laden with blooms. The plants have been potted in simple jugs and vases from the kitchen for a relaxed look to reflect the mood of the occasion.

flowers and plants **45**

A cymbidium orchid stem looks dramatic immersed in an over-sized glass vase. Change the water frequently and occasionally cut down the stem, and your orchid should last a long time.

Instead of opting for the traditional Christmas tree, try decorating cacti or other large indoor plants. Re-pot the plants in galvanized buckets and string them with festive fairy lights.

Don't forget artificial flowers – they are particularly good value as they can be used time and time again, and are excellent for a lively party setting or a kitsch and colourful themed occasion. Pull the petals away from each flower head to scatter over the table, or simply float the complete head in a bowl.

The elements of lighting, flowers and plants can be put together very effectively. Float flower heads and petals together with floating candles in a large bowl on the table and try wrapping fairy lights around potted plants. Place a thick pillar candle in a storm lantern, wind light or hurricane lamp and stuff petals and flower heads around the sides to form a floral 'bed' at the base of the candle. A string of electric lights wound around a tall potted cactus, cheese plant or money plant will create an interesting light 'sculpture', perfect for festive occasions, such as a modern-themed Christmas event or a New Year's Eve drinks party.

An inexpensive option for flowers on the table is to fill a vase or dish with water and float colourful petals or flower heads. These chrysanthemum heads have been dyed with blue colouring and look wonderful floating amongst blue gel candles. This would make a perfect party table centrepiece – and talking point! Use variations of this idea to create areas of colour and light on the table.

below Add slices of lime to the water in your ice-cube tray for drinks that are both refreshing and attractive.
right Traditional, practical glassware is always the best. This simple juicer is on hand for immediate fresh juice, which can be stored in a milk bottle for breakfast time. The coloured elements here are highlighted by the use of glass items.
opposite left Keep interesting packaging collected on your travels. These colourful tins are useful for containing straws or cutlery.
opposite right Interesting centrepieces can be built up from found objects. These shells were collected from the beach and strung together to wind around a tin plate laden with watermelon.

all the extras

Introduce any items that catch your eye and could serve as vessels for food, candles or flowers. These often bring the most special touches to the table.

Often the most original and inventive pieces are found on a lazy Sunday morning wandering around a car-boot sale or spotted in the window of a local charity shop. You may be away on holiday and happen to spy the most perfect soapstone bowl in a local craft shop or stroll along the beach and look down onto a cluster of interesting shells. All these items have their turn somewhere and will come out at the opportune moment – just remember that you have them and keep them close to hand.

Look out for plates and dishes that can be used as centrepieces – interesting wooden or tin trays and bowls or maybe a length of textured slate or cork to present condiments. Any pieces that can be used as storage vessels are worth considering for the table top, too – reuse tins and jars for sugar, cutlery, bread, flowers, and so on. It is all these little extras that give your setting an individual and unique edge, which your guests will appreciate and remember.

There are many festive occasions to inspire a special table setting, but sometimes it is just as enjoyable to make a celebration of a gathering with friends or a quiet evening in at home. The occasion or event can be your starting point for the theme of the table setting, such as working with eggs at Easter, or a traditional gold and red Christmas. Equally, inspiration can start with a bunch of favourite flowers, a special length of fabric that you'd like to use across the table, or some new floating candles to experiment with.

the occasions

right This sunny breakfast setting is enhanced by sticking to a palette of yellows and oranges, with the strong spots of blue from the practical paper napkins.
below These colourful handmade egg cups are ideal for holding coarse sea salt to pass around the breakfast table. You can also use spare egg cups for individual servings of butter and jam at each setting.

weekday breakfast

For a weekday start, food needs to be fast, and you will want to offer family and guests a range of healthy options.

An early morning meal needs a setting that is practical, informal – and appealing enough to get out of bed for! Liven up the breakfast table with fresh, bold colours. Gather just a few colourful stems, such as ranuncula or large daisies, fresh from the garden. They will look great adorning the table, arranged simply in recycled bottles and jars, adding splashes of colour to your table top.

Clean, practical glassware looks good on the kitchen table and can be mixed and matched for an interesting setting. Be inventive with your use of simple kitchen items to serve food – use small plain glass pots to hold a choice of jam and marmalade, and decant breakfast cereals into storage jars. A tin mug makes an interesting cornflake scoop and colourful egg cups are just the right size for individual salt containers.

By carefully choosing the packaging of food elements, such as milk cartons and condiment pots, you can further stylize this type of setting. Employ paper napkins and pots of ready-made yoghurt

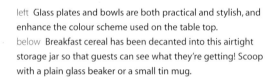

left Glass plates and bowls are both practical and stylish, and enhance the colour scheme used on the table top.
below Breakfast cereal has been decanted into this airtight storage jar so that guests can see what they're getting! Scoop with a plain glass beaker or a small tin mug.

to save on time and washing-up! Opt for individual glass pots of French yoghurt (these can be reused later for homemade yoghurt) and always have a pot of runny honey to hand.

A mobile trolley laden with breakfast foods keeps the table top clear and can be wheeled between the eaters. You can use this to hold newspapers and magazines for easy access and to build up a collection of delicious jams and marmalades for friends and family to take their pick. Just wipe down the trolley and tidy it up ready to wheel it out again the next morning. Bags of coffee, sugar, cereal and bread can be resealed with colourful pegs, without the need to use plastic film or storage containers.

Stick to easy options for a weekday breakfast. That way, you will be able to enjoy your meal without feeling rushed.

right For a finishing touch, pop into the garden and pick some fresh blooms. These recycled glass milk bottles make interesting vases for single stems of ranuncula.
below Look out for interesting food packaging that can be displayed on the table top. This Chinese honey pot looks great in this setting.

right Keep bags of bread and cereals and packets of freshly ground coffee airtight by clipping with cheap-and-cheerful plastic pegs. This will keep them fresh and ready for latecomers to the breakfast table.

this page Individual pots of French yoghurt
look stylish at this breakfast spread. Keep
the glass pots after the event and reuse
with homemade or decanted yoghurt, or
to hold candles at another occasion. Keep
an abundance of paper napkins to hand
and there will be no need for plates.

lazy weekend breakfast

Start the day with a wholesome breakfast over which family and friends can chat, relax and plan the rest of the weekend.

A generous linen tablecloth provides an excellent base for a big breakfast. Throw this over a good-sized kitchen table and lay out enough china and cutlery for your guests to indulge in whatever they fancy from your spread.

Start with basic but versatile china and accessories. The elements of a practical kitchen are ideal – plenty of uncomplicated glassware and simple, white china. Look out for dual-purpose tableware, too: if you are offering boiled eggs, why not try reusing napkin rings as egg cups? And have fun with your settings. For example, personalize the boiled eggs before laying them out by simply jotting a guest's name on the shell in pencil. Or fill individual pots with butter, cool and simply carve out a name or initial with a skewer to mark each place. Make sure there is plenty of tea and coffee available – and don't fight over the newspapers!

opposite left Layer china at each setting with different-sized plates and top with a tall glass filled with yoghurt and cereal.

opposite right Dig out individual glass jars for marmalade and pour fresh fruit juice into measuring jugs. Dried apricots are excellent on cereal or just to nibble – and they match the colour scheme, too!

left Bright flowers such as sunflowers or big daisies in tall jars are perfect for a sunny breakfast.

above Offer a choice of teas and coffees in labelled pots.

this page **The perfect setting for Sunday brunch! Aim to position your guests with a view out to the garden or at least by a window. That way they can check on what the weather is doing and make plans for the rest of the day.**

indulgent brunch

A table laid for a generous brunch is a perfect place to spend a long lazy Sunday, relaxing with your family and friends.

Choose a selection of plain white china and a full set of silver or stainless-steel cutlery to give a clean fresh look to the table top. Lay out an abundance of glassware to allow for plenty of water, juice, wine and spicy Bloody Marys! A jar of mixed olives added to the line-up of glasses at each setting will provide something to nibble with a pre-brunch drink while guests get comfortable. Finally, place cappuccino coffee cups and saucers at each setting, so that everything is to hand and the coffee can be passed around the table.

Single stems of flowers work well at this style of setting. You want to give a splash of fresh colour while still keeping the main body of the table top clear for the other elements. Cymbidium orchids are ideal. Though relatively expensive, a single stem goes a long way – and will look fresh for a long

left **Each place setting is carefully labelled and laid out in the same way. Create order before the chaos ensues!**
above **Look out for vases in interesting shapes and start building up a versatile collection.**

time. Pluck off the lower orchid heads complete with their short stems, place each in water in an individual jar (tealight holders or shot glasses are ideal) and put one jar at each place setting. Luggage labels or price tickets can then be tied to each jar or stem to act as namecards – brunch is a good occasion to mix up different groups of friends in an informal atmosphere. Keep the remaining orchid blooms on the longer stem for a taller plain-glass vase in the centre of the table.

Lay the china, glassware and cutlery in a neat and formal way and then top each setting with something tasty, such as a breakfast bagel or muffin. The overall look of the setting should be orderly and smart to avoid the table becoming 'messy' with all the different types of foods your guests will be eating. You can soften down the hard shapes of the china and cutlery with central clusters of decorative glass beads or pebbles. Once the food is put out, everything will be to hand, and guests and hosts can relax together.

shore-side picnic

Lay out a picnic on wooden decking overlooking a busy estuary, where you can watch the fishing boats come in and out while indulging in a delicious seaside feast.

A more relaxed buffet-style spread is usually the best layout for this event. Let guests choose what they would like to eat and make sure there are plenty of napkins and cutlery to hand.

Fold napkins – plain linen or squares of denim are ideal, but paper napkins are very convenient – and put them in separate bundles with a knife and fork. Tie each bundle with a small luggage label so that guests can rummage for their own cutlery.

Rather than adding herbs directly to a large salad, create a miniature, portable herb garden in a seed tray or large serving dish, so guests can help themselves to a fresh garnish. Ideal plants are parsley, rosemary, coriander, basil, mint or chives. See what is available at the local supermarket or garden centre.

Make sure there is plenty of fresh chilled mineral water available. Prepare dishes of frozen fruit – slices of lime, lemon and orange are great to flavour the water and keep it cool.

opposite left Be inventive with your containers for cutlery and food. Why not use little metal buckets to hold cutlery and save tin cans for breadsticks and nuts, to fit in with the relaxed, outdoor holiday feel?

opposite right Put a selection of three or four herb plants in a galvanized tray. Look after your portable garden and it can be brought out again and again.

right Lay out the buffet elements across the ground. A large strip of raffia or a tablecloth folded lengthways makes an excellent 'base' for your picnic setting.

below When preparing food away from home, make good use of the natural objects, like shells and stones, you find around your picnic site.

Be inspired by your surroundings and incorporate natural elements from your picnic site into your table setting.

beach barbecue

Pack plenty of food and drink for a day at the beach. As the shadows start to lengthen, light the barbecue – and enjoy!

If you are planning a cook-out at the beach, invest in a disposable barbecue – it is by far the easiest option. Surround it with large pebbles for decoration and added safety. If the meal is going to be a big event, with lots of hungry mouths to feed, then a whole row of barbecues set up like this will look great.

Paper plates and napkins are the simplest option, as they can all be thrown into a big rubbish bag at the end of the meal. Peg each plate together with a napkin and cutlery, and supply tin mugs as lightweight drinking vessels.

A washing-up bowl can be used as a large ice bucket for food and drinks. Bring a bag of ice and let it slowly melt down in the bowl, or sit the bowl firmly in the sand where the sea will lap around it and keep drinks cool. Make sure you pack plenty of storage jars filled with nuts, dried fruit and other snacks to nibble on through the afternoon. They can be reused when empty to transport any left-over food home.

Finally, remember to take lanterns and cosy blankets for when the sun goes down. Bring out flasks of warming soup and there will be no need to hurry home.

opposite A barbecue on the beach – what a treat! Make sure you take everything you need so you are set up for the day. Disposable paper plates and napkins are a must. A big beach blanket, a radio and lots of reading matter are necessities, and take a few lanterns to find your way back through the dunes in the dark!

below A napkin, a straw, a fork and a paper plate are all held together with a useful wooden peg to give as a complete bundle to each guest.

top Breadsticks are tied in a bundle with string and a denim tea towel has been rolled up and secured with a length of twine and a shell.

above A large aluminium bowl makes a practical carrier for food and can be used as a drinks chiller once you arrive at your picnic spot.

mediterranean-style table

Prepare an alfresco lunch on the terrace, combining deep blue with white and accents of bright bougainvillaea – for a look evoking summer holidays spent beside the Mediterranean.

You don't need a large garden for open-air dining. Any outdoor space will do, as long as there is enough room for a table! Whitewashed wood and old garden furniture are ideal surfaces to build up a Mediterranean-themed setting, but any table will do. Try a sturdy pasting table if you don't have any garden furniture, and cover it with a large cloth.

Stick to a colour scheme of Mediterranean tones, using white, bright pink and sea blue. The best table elements for this theme are chunky glassware, preferably

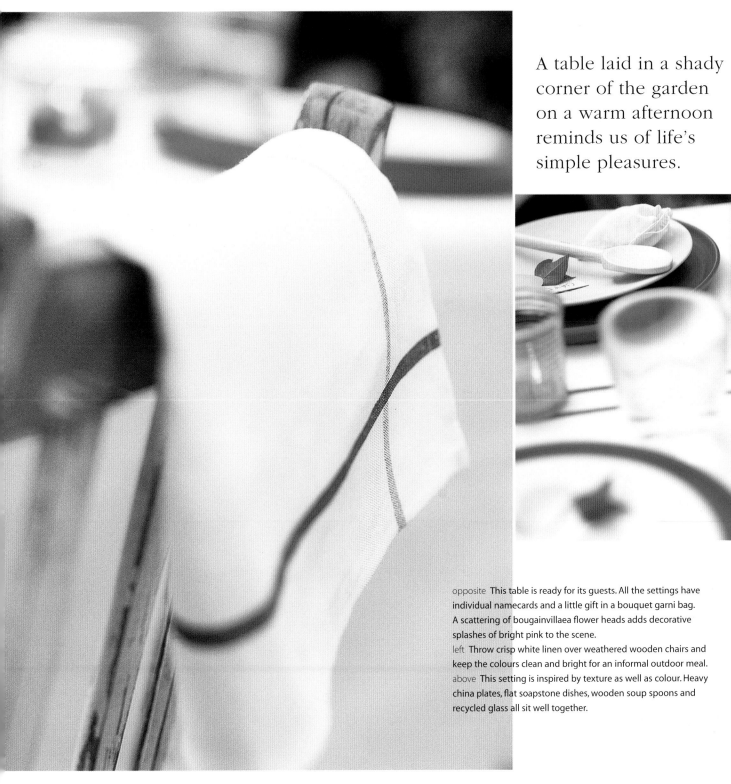

A table laid in a shady corner of the garden on a warm afternoon reminds us of life's simple pleasures.

opposite **This table is ready for its guests. All the settings have individual namecards and a little gift in a bouquet garni bag. A scattering of bougainvillaea flower heads adds decorative splashes of bright pink to the scene.**
left **Throw crisp white linen over weathered wooden chairs and keep the colours clean and bright for an informal outdoor meal.**
above **This setting is inspired by texture as well as colour. Heavy china plates, flat soapstone dishes, wooden soup spoons and recycled glass all sit well together.**

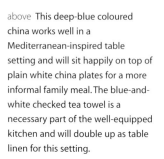

above **This deep-blue coloured china works well in a Mediterranean-inspired table setting and will sit happily on top of plain white china plates for a more informal family meal. The blue-and-white checked tea towel is a necessary part of the well-equipped kitchen and will double up as table linen for this setting.**

right Dangle lanterns from any available branch or wall. The version shown here is big enough to hold a larger candle that will stay lit for hours. Make your own lanterns from discarded glass jam jars – just wash thoroughly, remove the labels and hang them in groups around your Mediterranean setting.

Whatever the occasion, have fun with the table top by putting extra thought into the presentation and the surrounding environment.

the thick, recycled variety, and a mixture of china in soapstone and matt ceramic. If you have any blue pieces, mix them with white china and stick to plain white candles.

If your outdoor space is lacking in colour and foliage, invest in colourful additions, such as bougainvillaea, or bring out house plants for the day to liven up the scene. Re-pot them in aluminium buckets, galvanized containers and large terracotta pots to create your Mediterranean environment, and remove loose petals to scatter over the table. Any old buckets that aren't full of flowers can be used to hold pebbles or floating candles, so that your theme is taken beyond the table top.

Even if it is daylight when you eat, it is always special to have candles on the table, and it means that your guests can sit around until the light goes down. Lanterns are fun, too, and perfect to ensure candles stay alight in the breeze when dining outdoors. They can be hung from surrounding branches and fencing. Choose smaller jars for little candles and be inventive with what the candles are 'planted' in. White sand, gravel or dishwasher salt is ideal. Look out for chips of coloured mosaic glass – often found in florists and craft shops. Pet shops and aquatic suppliers stock coloured sand in shades of pink and blue that are also suitable for a Mediterranean-style table.

right A miniature cacti garden is an unusual 'centrepiece'. It has been made by setting tiny pots of cacti in a bed of white gravel scattered with blue glass mosaic.
below Chips of coloured glass mosaic have been put in the base of candleholders to spread colour across the table.

A fresh, modern approach to decorating the table will ensure happy guests and encourage good conversation.

modern chic dining

With a little inspiration, and a minimum of fuss, you can turn a simple meal with friends into a really special occasion.

At this sort of gathering, seat guests at the ends of the table as well as along the sides, so everyone can scan the table as a whole. Lay each place setting with a basic knife, fork and spoon and a large platter, then play around with china and use beakers and saucers for dessert. Rather than using a tablecloth, keep things simple by laying each setting on an individual placemat.

Steel and aluminium will sit well with this contemporary look. Search for little metal cases for candles or sit tealights in pie cases, and use seed trays or a planter for the centrepiece. Vegetables can be as attractive as fruit or flowers on the table, and succulent plants will fit well in this environment, so try piling the central planter with interesting shapes, such as gourds or artichoke heads – these can be cooked for dinner the next day!

Raw materials, like slate, will also complement this minimal setting. Slate placemats are widely available and can double up as chalkboards. You could put a piece at each place setting and chalk

opposite and left **Stick to a neutral colour scheme – natural earthenware, plain-styled cutlery and clear, simple glassware complement raw materials like wood and slate.**
below **Use the slate placemats to start a table game between courses.**

this page **This cool modern table setting is perfect for a lunch-time gathering. Settings are marked out neatly with placemats, and a large versatile platter at each setting holds a napkin and napkin ring. A centrepiece of large artichoke heads makes an unusual but stylish impact. A bowl of fruit would also have worked well – guests could then have helped themselves for dessert.**

Pale wood, white Formica and cool shades of green all work towards the light, airy feel.

out your guests' names, or simply use the slate for games. A less expensive alternative that will work just as well is to buy chopping boards or squares of plywood and paint them with blackboard paint.

Keep glassware simple, but be inventive with namecards. Cards can be spiked down onto bamboo skewers or cocktail sticks to indicate seating arrangements.

A perfect setting for this meal is a minimal dining room or a large modern stainless-steel kitchen, but don't feel restricted by your environment. Simply clear away as much clutter from the room as possible for a fresh, contemporary feel, or adapt the table decoration to take in inspiration from the rest of the room. Sticking to a neutral palette with shades of grey and green will keep this setting fresh and relaxed, while the odd floating candle and pairs of glowing votives dotted over the table top remind guests that it is a special occasion.

above Floating candles gently illuminate the corners of the table and introduce the element of water to the setting. They have been layered by placing the bowls on small linen coasters to coordinate with the placemats. A bamboo skewer becomes an inventive namecard spike, and a handy piece of lime sits below for both decoration and practicality.

above left A piece of slate becomes a useful condiment tray. The oil and vinegar have been decanted into recycled glass jars and can be poured back after the meal or resealed for later.

asian-style banquet

Don't worry if you don't have a dining table, as a low surface, such as a coffee table, is an excellent starting point for an oriental-inspired meal. Search your home for cushions to scatter on the floor around the table for low-level seating.

Eating at a low-level dining area, seated on silk cushions, will give you a really decadent, oriental feel. If you make your own cushions, buy enough material for a matching panel at the window.

Simple, heavy linen over the table top, or a long raffia mat, will provide a good base on which to build. Choose simple shapes in basic neutral colours and add splashes of bright colour with suitable flowers – magenta-coloured Singapore orchids are ideal here and, once again, you can economize by plucking lower flower heads to float singly. Pale duck-egg blue and sage green will also go well with this muted palette. Pull up a nearby bench to stack any extra china necessary for the following courses – this will help keep the table top clear and uncomplicated.

Have a good look around an oriental food store for individual bottles of drink to put in place of glasses at each setting. There are fun packages of fruit juice to be found and little bottles of saki will also work well. Individual glass bottles can also be effectively reused for flowers or chilled water at another occasion. Try lining up a multiple row of bottles along the length of the table and pop a single stem of decorative grass in each.

opposite top Create a 'centrepiece' from a large dish or tray holding unusual dishes and bottles of soy sauce and oil for guests to help themselves to.
below left and opposite main The strong graphic lines characteristic of an Asian theme are relaxed with the addition of small pots and bowls for flowers, candles and seeds.
below Stick to the basics – a noodle bowl, napkin and chopsticks – at each place.

lunch on the lawn

Taking your lunch out into the garden is always a special treat. Here, even the simplest of salads deserves a well-considered setting.

Soften the look of a metal garden table with a loosely woven piece of plain linen. This will blow in the breeze for a fresh, floaty, romantic look, perfect for a bright summer's day lunch, and will work equally well for a balmy early evening supper.

Keep the colour scheme simple and uncomplicated, using neutrals and shades of white. Natural elements, such as soapstone, raw linen and dried flower heads, will fit in well with the setting. Take inspiration from your surroundings for colours and materials, using delicately coloured flowers on the table top, and grasses (such as bear grass and snake grass) to tie around rolled napkins or beakers.

A plain church candle will provide a simple centrepiece and an ice-filled vase makes a cooling water-bottle holder. Lay each place setting with a simple large dish and a single fork to enjoy a

A couple of soft pink garden blooms add spots of colour to this understated alfresco dining area, without competing with the colours of the summer garden all around. The flowers sit in simple tall glass jars or clear-glass water bottles, and decorative butterflies perch on the edge of each wineglass.

Make the most of a breezy, summer afternoon by carrying a table onto the lawn and serving a crisp salad.

summer salad. Fold plain linen napkins down to coaster size and place them under water beakers. Feel inspired to mix cooling summer drinks. Cut up tiny cubes of lemon and lime and add them to your ice-cube tray when you fill it. These will look and taste fabulous in a glass of sparkling mineral water.

Linen is the perfect fabric for a tablecloth and napkins at this event. A bleached denim would look equally good outside, especially if an ugly table has to be hidden away. Plain unbleached cotton muslin fabric is also an inexpensive way to cover an alfresco table.

Soapstone looks good in a natural, neutral setting, but bleached wooden bowls would work equally well, and remember those glass plates if you need to lay your hands on extra pieces that won't dominate the general ambience of the table top. Choose thick chunky glass, preferably recycled, and, if you can't decant your drinks, stick to sympathetic mineral-water packaging, as these bottles are often made from recycled glass themselves, with attractive minimal labels.

Hang simple lanterns made from recycled jam jars from surrounding branches so that your meal can last into dusk.

above left This table is very simply laid, with lots of natural elements, such as loosely woven raw linen, soapstone platters and recycled glass. The soapstone beakers and vase (which is used here to hold the water bottle) have practical value, too, as the stone's insulating properties will keep cold drinks cool on a hot afternoon.

opposite right Each place has its own little dish of sea salt and coarsely ground black pepper to sprinkle over the salad if desired. A dried flower head is a delicate addition to the setting.

this page A strand of bear grass has been carefully tied around the beaker for a decorative touch. A plain linen napkin is presented in a new way, by folding it and sitting it beneath the beaker.

eastern-style elegance

Be experimental with colour for an elegant, Asian-themed party. It's fun to mix strong colours together on the table top.

Coloured cut glass works well within this theme. Scour antique shops and markets for interesting pieces. Don't worry if you only manage to find single glasses, as they can be used as unusual tealight holders or mixed with other odd pieces for a more bohemian look. Find a sumptuous piece of fabric to use as a runner or tablecloth and choose napkins that will work well with it. Experiment with folding them in different ways and, for a change, try placing them under the plates.

Place a row of plants along the centre of the table lengthwise. If possible, re-plant them in bowls that match the dinner service you are using. Orchids are ideal for an Asian theme: their roots are reasonably shallow and the plants can be easily transferred and reused in other table settings. Try to pick plants with a deep colour to their flowers that mixes well with the other coloured table elements.

opposite left   Mix materials around the table. Silver beakers reflect surrounding colours for an interesting surface effect that brings everything together visually.

opposite right   The thin stem of an orchid is perfect for a table situation, where guests won't want to peer at each other through bushy plants.

above   Be decorative with foliage, too – an interesting leaf will give texture to a side plate – but be sure to avoid any poisonous varieties!

right   Draw inspiration from fabrics and furnishings around your home. A length of unusual fabric makes a great runner. Pick out colours from this to reflect in your choice of elements.

cool classic dining

A formal occasion calls for an elegant table top with lots of crisp white linen, fine china and sparkling glassware.

It's always a pleasure to have the chance to do something special with table settings, and a formal dinner gives you the perfect opportunity. If you are using an everyday dining surface, opt for a starched white tablecloth or placemats. If you have neither of these, then why not use well-ironed clean white napkins to mark out each place at the table? If the napkins cover more than the width of the table when placed opposite each other, think of each pair as a runner across the surface and allow them to overhang the edges of the table.

Flowers and foliage can be most effective when they are kept to a minimum. Here, the odd frond of fern in a simple vase will be just enough to accentuate the clean, starched look. Carefully consider shapes at this table and choose vases that won't detract from the setting as a whole. A low, round vase is ideal, as is a spherical fishbowl shape. If you are short of vases,

right A beaded napkin ring is a decadent namecard holder, and gel candles mix well with fine glassware.
opposite Warm candlelight gives a magical glow that extends over the mantelpiece and sideboard, combining with the soft fern fronds to bring a subtle elegance to the occasion.

Choose classic simple shapes for stylish elegance
and keep everything to a minimum.

substitute with a plain clear bottle or a clean decanter. Pick out the green of the foliage with fresh fruit that can be offered after the meal – pears and green apples will always fit into an elegant setting and sit decoratively in a stemmed dish or plain white ceramic fruit bowl.

Keep the atmosphere clean but moody with lots of little table candles. Plain metal-cased nightlights are ideal and can be set in neat lines around the table. Look out for small plain-glass votive holders, too, that will add to the minimal feel. Invest in some glass droplets or larger hollow balls (available from florists and gift shops) to sit between the candles or in clusters in glass bowls. The abundance of clean clear glass will give your table ultimate elegance.

By using minimal colours and simple elements, you will accentuate the shapes laid out on the table top. Play around with this idea and try to offset the circular shapes of china and glassware with harder lines of cutlery and linen. So long as the elements involved in this elegant setting are uniform, they needn't be expensive. It is the clean lines and overall orderliness of the presentation that will give it a 'smart' look.

left Pairs of well-starched linen placemats have been joined together to lie across the table and gently drape over each side. A matching napkin sits along the back of each chair.
opposite main Between the lines of white linen, rows of hollow glass balls have been interspersed with tealights, accentuating the glowing spots of light.

below A plain-glass dip tray found at a charity shop makes an excellent dish for nibbles.

bottom left This is a very graphic setting, with lots of circular objects set out in orderly lines. The minimal fern fronds give it a hint of softness; cool white calla lilies would have fitted in well here, too.

exotic finger-food feast

Go to town with colour and prepare for an exotic-styled meal. Set a low table with rich fabrics and scatter plenty of comfortable cushions for guests to sit on.

Think of exotic, far-flung lands and feel inspired. Gather up plenty of different-sized cushions from around the house and make simple slip covers for them from bright satin fabric – lining fabric works well, too, and can be found cheaply at markets. Make sure there's plenty left over to be used to make a set of napkins and a table runner in coordinating colours.

Exotic flowers are ideally suited to this occasion, but colourful gerbera and carnations will look just as good, and will cost far less. Float the flower heads in small coloured bowls dotted about the table top. Clean glass tealight holders or Moroccan tea glasses make perfect drinking beakers for wine and fruit juice. Decant coloured liquids into interesting vessels and empty bottles. Why not try adding a drop of grenadine or coloured fruit cordial to mineral water for a special exotic-looking drink?

Don't worry too much about the practicality of eating a full meal at this type of setting. Offer a selection of bread in a dark wooden bowl or marble dish, provide lots of finger food … and make sure there are plenty of napkins to hand!

left Use candles and fairy lights to illuminate your dining area. Be inventive: a bright sheet or scarf makes an excellent tablecloth. And try sitting fairy lights under a glass-topped table to create an interesting glow through your tablecloth.
below Cut up slices of exotic fruit to offer to your guests and to decorate the table top. Guests will have fun testing and sharing new flavours.

this page, main Low-hanging lights, such as coloured glass Indian and Moroccan lanterns, add to the warmth and intimacy of the occasion and are easily illuminated with single tealights.

this page, inset Tiny coloured glass bowls hold floating flower heads in bright hues. These look very exotic against the richly coloured pashmina that has been used to cover the table.

romantic meal for two

Plan ahead and get everything ready so that you can unplug the
phone, relax and enjoy each other's undivided attention.

A special romantic table setting is suitable for all sorts of occasions. Obvious
opportunities are Valentine's Day or an anniversary, but this is also an enjoyable
table to set up for a quiet birthday meal or to celebrate a promotion at work. Or
why not just celebrate being romantic?

Red is a good – and traditional – colour for romantic liaisons and can look
stunning mixed with everyday glassware. Choose modern functional table
elements to brighten up the setting and use plain red napkins – fabric or paper,
depending on the 'smartness' of the occasion. Simple square napkins can be
easily made at home from red cotton fabric, but paper napkins often add an
interesting twist to an indoor meal.

Decorate the table top with little gifts that fit in with the occasion. Find
photographs to remind you both of special times. Miniature chocolates are a nice

above left The look needn't be dark and heavy to create an
intimate setting. This bright studio apartment dresses up well for
a romantic meal. The colour red has been spread around the room
– and is even extended to the window boxes! Red and green work
particularly well together and here are accentuated in the choice
of elements – the glassware, china and flowers – all set off
perfectly by the simple glass table top.

above A collection of candles has been grouped together,
displayed in a variety of tealight holders and everyday glasses
to match the red-and-green colour scheme. These will all be lit
as the evening grows darker.

left Try layering plain glass plates with coloured china and choose cutlery with coloured handles or use bright chopsticks. Chopsticks can be bought in a variety of colours or you can paint them yourself, using non-toxic paint.
below Collect tealight holders in clean bright colours and recycle them as individual salt and pepper pots.

this page The table has been decorated with a mixture of carefully picked items. Miniature twinkling fairy lights are intertwined around spiky grass plants. Sticks with a display of bright-red feathers were found at a local florist and can be used to stir cocktails. A strand of bear grass ties the chopsticks together and a fig sits on a carefully layered stack of china and glass.

Any day can become a romantic occasion …
make the most of your time together.

surprise, as are individual bottles of brightly coloured drink, such as Campari. Drink cranberry juice or add grenadine to wine or sparking water for more colour, and choose exotic fruit, such as figs or dates, as an attractive starter.

Another chance to bring colour and texture to the table is to tie cutlery or chopsticks together. Use thick strands of grass or clusters of feathers with a wired malleable end and keep a store of beads or buttons to tie around glassware.

Cacti and grasses will look interesting and unusual at this setting – that is, if you're not opting for red roses! Use plain-glass mixing bowls for pots and sit the plants on beds of white gravel or stones. Miniature fairy lights are relatively easy to come by and can be twisted into potted plants to jazz up the table lighting. If the table is by a window, then extend your inspiration to colourful window boxes, to blend the setting in with the rest of the room.

above left A card-holder is a fun way to present namecards. Dig out old photographs of the two of you and share happy memories.
above Glassware can be basic and is made decorative with the simple addition of a coloured plastic heart attached with thin jewellery wire. Miniature bottles of drinks are a special touch at each place setting. Aim to colour-coordinate these, too.

above The clean modern lines of this classic glass table and leather chairs make a great base to build a Father's Day spread. Colours have been kept reasonably masculine, with dark stoneware and grey felt placemats and coasters. The yellow glassware makes an interesting combination.

father's day spread

Father's Day offers an opportunity to present a more masculine style of setting, which would also be suitable for a formal occasion, such as a business lunch.

Aim to set the table in a 'smart' way, led by your father's favourite colours. Heavy dark china will sit well with colourful glassware and give a modern look to the setting.

A glass-topped table is an excellent base to show off these different textures and colours. Felt is also an interesting surface to work on and can be easily cut to the shape of the table top if you want to disguise it – dark brown or grey are good colours to opt for. A simple linen runner will soften and protect a glass table – if you are making your own, then why not combine two colours so that you have different-coloured ends, and make matching napkins in alternate colours? For a set of four napkins, choose two colours and make two napkins predominantly one colour with a coordinating stripe; and vice versa for the second pair.

Protect your table top with mats and coasters. Leather, fleece and felt are all good materials to cut up into simple shapes. Add interest by using pinking shears around the edges or cut central holes or initials into the mats.

main A bundle of bamboo stalks tied with a strand of bear grass decorates each place setting. The drinking glasses have been placed upside down for a change and a little pre-wrapped packet of biscuits is laid to the right of the setting for each guest.
above right A plain-glass votive holder has been wrapped with a piece of oriental paper to give an interesting glow.
above far right A square tank vase makes an ideal deep vessel for a selection of olives. Sit them stylishly on pieces of banana leaf.

Fine glassware sits with heavy china for a masculine feel. The glass table top ensures that all colours are seen clearly.

Lay plates give a neat ordered look to the table and are useful for resting bread and cutlery. The cutlery should be smart and simple, sticking to the minimum number of utensils needed on the table.

Individual salt shakers are fun, and namecards sit well in the collection of elements at each place. Add pre-dinner nibbles at each setting, too, in the form of decorative table treats. Scour oriental supermarkets for crisps or biscuits in interesting packaging.

Experiment with ways of presenting glassware –

stack pieces, lay them upside down and mix different sizes of tumblers. Wrapping simple glass votive holders will add interest to the table lighting. Chinese and Japanese paper are ideal, and tissue and crepe paper also work well. Combine these with floating candles in circular dishes or interesting ashtrays.

Choose minimal stems, such as blossom, pussy willow and bamboo, to stand in vases on the table and surrounding areas. These will last for a long time and don't need much looking after.

above A namecard nestles in each bowl alongside an interesting salt shaker. The white china looks great against the darker stoneware.
above left Decant red wine into a plain glass decanter, put this amongst the other metal- and glassware, and watch all the reflections work together on the table top.

All the colours on this table work extremely well together. Don't be afraid of using dark shades – as long as the setting is lightened up with the occasional piece of bright glassware. The oriental paper with gold-leaf decoration that has been wrapped around the votive holders gives a special glow that also livens up the surrounding glass elements.

Flowers are a good starting point for a Mother's Day setting. Pick out soft pastel shades of colour inspired by seasonal sweet peas, peonies and pansies.

mother's day treat

A Mother's Day lunch is a good opportunity to bring out any special pieces of china and glassware. Dainty glass plates and softly toned drinking glasses look elegant laid out on a special tablecloth. Mix and match these at each place setting and use them to display sweets, cakes, sandwiches, fruit and flowers on the table top. Silver or clear acrylic-handled cutlery will also work well in this setting. And select napkins in different shades from the same palette.

Don't be afraid to mix different colours and styles of glassware, linen and cutlery. So long as you stick to the same soft colour palette and don't overload the table, it will all look good together. By using more glassware, you will pick up subtle colours and keep the table looking fresh. Larger apothecary jars look great with pastel-coloured after-dinner bonbons or simply filled with scrunched-up tissue paper to bring more areas of colour to the table top and surrounding surfaces.

opposite and left **The pastel colours of the flowers and table linen, along with the dainty pieces of glassware, make this an excellent setting for a Mother's Day lunch.** below **For a pretty display, float hollow glass beads in a glass bowl amongst softly coloured petals and flower heads.**

Choose her favourite flower for the theme of the whole table setting.

Look out for prettily packaged cakes and biscuits for this Mother's Day treat. Scour your local delicatessen for unusual desserts and place these on a fine glass platter or special china plate on the centre of the table top to be lit by a ring of pretty tealights in clear glass holders. It needn't be expensive to look good in this setting!

Be inventive with flowers. Lay the table near an open window, where you can enjoy natural light and extend your pretty colour scheme around the room and beyond, with flowers on the mantelpiece and windowsill and tiny jars of candles hanging from bright ribbon. Cottage-garden flowers are ideal and can be displayed in lots of ways. Re-plant pansies in recycled jugs and vases to decorate the area around the table. Pull petals from sweet peas and other delicate flowers to float in glass vases and continue the colours around the room. A single carnation head holds a wealth of petals that can be separated and floated in glass bowls of water.

Everyone appreciates a table gift, so indulge your guests with their own flowers at each setting. Choose pretty beakers to stand these in after tying with ribbon, so guests can take them away after the meal.

left Good-quality silverware is laid out next to a pretty bobble-edged plate all ready for Mother's Day tea time. Each place setting has its own miniature flower bouquet for the guests to take away with them. Softly coloured glass tumblers and patterned Moroccan tea glasses enhance the scheme, while a carefully chosen pre-packaged bottle of green tea sits happily amongst the decor.

top A miniature glass lantern hangs from a length of pink ribbon at the window next to the table.

above The beautifully packaged Italian dessert sits decoratively inside a ring of dainty glowing gel candles set out on a glass platter.

right An old wine bottle with a particularly attractive label makes an ideal vase for a full-headed peony. Sit this on the mantelpiece by a large mirror and you get two displays!

christening tea

Lay an informal table in the kitchen in soft, pastel tones. The overall look will be pretty and peaceful – perfect to welcome a new baby into the family.

A christening is a very special occasion among friends and family and is a wonderful excuse for a gathering. If you have a large kitchen table, make this the main base for the occasion and guests can roam around the rest of the house if they desire. If you are expecting a lot of visitors, then lay a themed buffet table; if you are having a smaller party, stick to a more simple table layout.

Pale pinks and blues are obvious colours for this event and will work well in a kitchen environment. If you have a solid wooden table, expose the bare wood and lay a series of runners across the width. Alternatively, lay the runners over a crisp white tablecloth. Cotton gingham is inexpensive and will look fresh and stylish on the table top. If you are making table runners yourself, you won't need much fabric for it to have an impact. Three pieces of gingham that just hang over

opposite left Pink gingham table runners provide a good base for this orderly setting. Cotton coasters and square glass candleholders sit alternately along the centre of the table and echo the geometric print of the runners underneath.

opposite right Practical and basic, French glass tumblers make great containers for sugar and sweets, and match the chosen colour scheme!

left Try using small bottle vases of different shapes together and place them in a line to contain similar-coloured displays of flowers.

below A pink candle sits in a bed of dishwasher salt.

opposite edges will suffice. Set up places opposite each other on the runners; the symmetry will fit well with the geometric fabric pattern. It's also fun to mix different sizes of gingham print, but try not to become too complicated – stick to either pink-and-white or blue-and-white checks. Napkins can be sewn from gingham or from plain pieces of cotton, which are then tied with gingham ribbon or strips of fabric left over from making the runners.

If you have any pastel-coloured china, now is the chance to use it. Basic everyday white china will also look good, as will practical glassware – look out for French tumblers and anything tinted slightly with the colours you have chosen.

Pale pink and white sweets and marshmallows are decorative and make excellent nibbles for adults and children alike. Put these in tumblers and display them in a row along the centre of the table in between glasses of water.

For pretty flower displays, mix individual stems such as miniature roses, lizianthus and eucalyptus, and use grasses to tie flowers together creatively.

children's party

Think bright and cheerful. Blow up a few balloons to trigger your inspiration for the party – this is one occasion when you can let your imagination run wild!

The kitchen is an ideal setting for a fun children's party. Here spillages don't matter too much and everything is on hand for serving food and clearing up. It is always good to have outdoor access, too, so party games can overflow into the garden.

The elements you employ needn't be expensive. Peel the labels off clear, plastic bottles and fill them with colourful drinks to help the effect – the way the food and drink looks is just as important as the way it tastes! Make placemats from craft felt or cut squares of bright carpet remnants or astroturf for a surreal effect kids will love.

Place a practical glass or metal bowl at each place setting (a basic mixing bowl will do) and pile it with goodies: a lunch box to eat from and pieces of dried fruit and other treats wrapped in plain-coloured paper tied with string. This will make the meal seem 'gift-like' for all concerned!

right Fairy lights adorned with artificial flowers will liven up the table and surrounding areas and are an especially good idea if you want to avoid using candles. A string of lights placed along the length of the table should give enough illumination without encroaching on individual settings.

Stick to a palette of bright primary colours for maximum 'wow' factor.

below To make sure all your guests take their seats, personalize each setting with imaginative namecards that children will really appreciate – here, Polaroid photographs were taken in the garden beforehand and then pegged to each bowl.
right Toy goldfish swimming in a large plastic bowl make an irresistible centrepiece.

above If you want to protect the table surface, then invest in a paper tablecloth and be sure to leave out lots of crayons to draw with. Paper tablecloths are available in a wide range of bright colours, which are bound to inspire little artists!

opposite Brightly coloured parrots sit on the back of each chair to welcome their guest! Each place setting is busy with colourful ideas to eat, drink and play with – perfect to entice young party-goers.

Prepare clear, plastic dishes of fruit jelly in lots of different colours for pudding and decorate the table with all the right party animals – rubber frogs, artificial goldfish and colourful toy parrots perched on the backs of the chairs.

Think of unusual party gifts for guests to take away. A miniature cactus at each setting will be fun and low-maintenance, but take care to plant them so that grabbing hands are safe from prickles. Foil take-away food containers or small boxes and bags can be personalized and filled with more goodies.

This is an opportunity to be as inventive as possible with your table setting. Just remember to stick to a bright colour palette and incorporate as many quirky pieces onto the table as you can. Peg, float, pot and place objects to keep your little guests happy and occupied throughout the party meal.

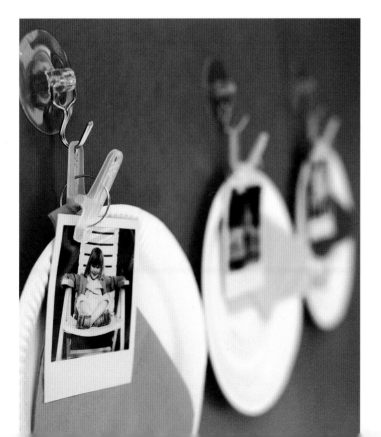

top Display bright flowers, such as gerbera, in plastic water bottles for fun.
above A blue frog, a potted cactus, a bowl of jelly, a square of grass and a host of irresistible packages – turn the tea table into a wonderland!
left Hang personalized paper plates and napkins along the wall, ready to be grabbed when the birthday cake comes out.

surprise birthday buffet

Buffets are ideal for parties. Choose the guest of honour's favourite colour as inspiration, and stick to it for everything you use – even the food!

A basic table or sideboard makes a good buffet surface. You could lay everything out over a stretch of kitchen work surface, but a free-standing table is the best option. Why not invest in a basic wallpaper-pasting table for this sort of event – then it can be easily be folded away and stored ready for the next occasion?

Decorate the area surrounding your buffet table in the same colour scheme. Hang decorations or paper lanterns above the table from a piece of ribbon suspended from each side of the room. Exploit your colour scheme further and

Choose your dominant colour, make your
second colour white, and add clear glassware
for maximum vibrancy on the table top.

opposite Everything here has been arranged
in groups for the guests to choose from.
Clear-glass tank vases are excellent to hold
both food and decorations. Candles in a
central vase can be lit as the party goes on
into the evening. A small bunch of carnations
makes a pretty token leaving gift.
left Single birthday candles have been placed
in individual meringues so that everyone gets
a birthday wish!
above A line of bright-pink vodka jellies sits
temptingly along the window ledge. Floral-
decorated fairy lights add a practical and fun
touch to the setting – keep these on all day
for spots of light.

this page, inset A line of Chinese paper lanterns accentuates the dominant colour choice at this party. Anything works, so long as it fits in with the scheme: a bright-pink bucket makes an ideal home for an orchid; and cartons of guava juice were chosen for their garish packaging. A length of wallpaper makes an interesting and practical table covering and sheets of vibrant paper add to the total layout.
this page, main Ricepaper flowers found in an oriental supermarket make a pretty buffet offering.

make coordinating jellies – vodka jellies if your guests are old enough! Choose sweets, candles, biscuits and paper plates to fit the scene and rummage around for extra decorative touches, such as feathers and artificial flowers.

Instead of overloading a single cake with birthday candles, plant them in individual meringues or cup cakes. If you are doing the baking yourself, remember the power of food colouring – a blue cake can be most alluring in the right setting! Decorate everyday glassware and plastic cups to fit in with your setting. Why not try stick-on bindis or use transfers? An extra-special and inexpensive idea is to prepare coloured ice cubes or, for a more subtle touch, add bright edible flower petals to your ice cube tray.

Candles of all shapes and sizes can be used at this event. You can stand candles in jars and tanks of sand or dishwasher salt if you do not have enough candlesticks – this looks effective with different shades of the same colour bunched up together. Fairy lights are a good choice for a birthday buffet, too. Hang them in clusters around the room, occasionally adding artificial flowers or rosettes of tissue paper to the flex (well away from the bulbs) to dress them in true party spirit!

above right This stemmed bowl holds party bags for each guest to take home with them. Make little gift bags for guests and fill them with special foil-wrapped chocolates or tiny gifts, such as pieces of jewellery. Pegs, pins or clips are ideal to seal the bags; decorate them with feathers and stick-on jewels.
right This large tealight sits inside a group of bangles for decoration. Tealights make inexpensive party lighting. Place them in groups around the room and decorate the metal cases with metallic ribbon or glitter.

Falling on a Sunday, Easter is a good day for a special lunch with family and friends. It also provides another great opportunity for themed table settings.

easter celebration

A palette of soft pastels lends itself well to this occasion. Work towards feminine shades of pale pink, green and blue, and introduce a layered theme with table linen. Textured natural linen is the ideal fabric for a table runner. If you want to make your own runner, buy a length of fabric long enough to drape slightly over the table ends and cut a suitable width. Hem along both long sides and gently fray the shorter edges to create a soft fringe. Use any spare fabric for matching napkins.

If you are having lots of guests and need to lay a large table, there's no need to own a complete set of matching china. Try mixing different-patterned china in similar colours. Pile plates together, starting with the dinner plate, then a smaller plate, and top with a dish or bowl for the starter. And, for a festive centrepiece, buy some tester pots of chalky pastel-coloured matt emulsion paint and decorate eggs to sit in small bowls and tall egg cups.

above The plates have been laid alternately in stripes and dots so no two settings opposite or alongside each other are the same.
right These eggs have been blown and painted in pastel shades to sit on a bed of silk and feathers as a decorative table piece.

this page **This table has been placed in the living room to be by the French windows leading to the garden for a quick egg-hunt-getaway after the meal! The surrounding areas – the side table and sofa – have also been decorated in the same colour scheme. Simple cushions made from plain raw silk add areas of brighter colour within the dreamy scheme.**

Touches of hot pink will liven up the pastel colour scheme. Look for lengths of pink ribbon and bright silk cushions to dot around to create more of a comfortable and informal setting suited to a family meal. Cushion covers in interesting textures can also be used as temporary seat covers.

This is a good opportunity to play with textures, incorporating chalky matt eggshells and delicate soft feathers. Everyone enjoys a festive occasion, so carry on the theme within individual settings, laying 'nests' for each guest and providing them with enough chocolate eggs to be getting on with before the main meal is served.

The combination of the airy linen tablecloth and pastel china and eggs gives an overall delicate and feminine feel to this occasion. And the humorous touches of fluffy feathers and chocolate eggs will appeal to guests young and old alike.

above For extra decoration at each setting, make individual 'nests' from rings of feathers to enclose ceramic or hard-boiled eggs.
above right Choose blooms in soft pinks and lilacs – peonies are ideal and pale-pink carnations will always look good. Carry the decorative theme through to the flowers by adding elements from the table, such as sticks with feathers tied to their tips.

Place the table by a large window or French doors overlooking the garden to view any prospective after-lunch egg hunts.

above Take inspiration from the occasion and incorporate feathers into the table setting. Table gifts are very fitting to a festive meal – try making individual egg 'nests' from plain-glass tealight holders and use double-sided tape to attach pure white feathers around the sides.

left Instead of formal namecards, use pretty ribbon to tie an old-fashioned luggage label to the back of each chair.

rustic halloween table

Try something a little different for Halloween and decorate a humble kitchen table with the fruits and colours of the season.

Get inspired by the colours of autumn – mustard, amber, oranges, reds, deep greens – and create a setting for a simple Halloween family meal. It's fun to have lots of relevant vegetation adorning the table for this themed occasion: gourds, artichokes, oranges and satsumas all work well together with the more traditional choice of pumpkins.

Enjoy the textures of the fruit and vegetables and try to reflect this in your selection of elements. If you have thick ceramic bowls and plates in different colours, now is the time to bring them out. Aim to unify the spread by sitting each bowl upon a lay plate – wood or rattan is ideal – or a rattan placemat. Build up layers of colour and don't be shy of using large fabric placemats with smaller woven mats on top – it will look good once the table is fully laid.

Think about your choice of cutlery, too. Nowadays there are many different styles to choose

opposite **As the evening draws in, this table will get more colourful with the glowing chilli lights and abundance of candles.** left and below **Everything on the table – placemats, bowls, glassware – echoes the shades of autumn!**

below and right Wooden dishes and bowls work well on a Halloween table. Use these to display groups of vegetables and place smaller dishes of nuts around the table for guests to nibble on between courses. Chopsticks come in all colours and shapes and can be used at the table for purely decorative purposes. Here they create a wonderful still life at each setting, combined with artichokes and gourds.

opposite Each place setting is surrounded with goodies. Here we see a tempting bowl full of nuts alongside a satsuma and a bottle of beer to ensure a happy guest!

from, with handles made of bamboo, wood, coloured resin and so on. Chopsticks can be colourful, too, placed alongside cutlery for variety and decoration or to be used for the starter. If you have basic steel or silver cutlery to hand, tie a colourful bow on the handle of the knife and place each whole setting on a richly coloured background.

Glassware in shades of red, orange, green and yellow will work really well on this table. Scour the supermarket for interesting green glass bottles of beer and sparkling mineral water. Choose candles in similar shades and make sure everything is glowing for a true Halloween experience. Bamboo-shaped candles and coloured tealights in coloured glass holders are perfect. Multicoloured fairy lights and outdoor lights will also be effective and encourage the festive spirit. If your table is by a window or doors leading outside, decorate the area you look onto with storm lanterns and lights. These will cast a spooky glow as the dark evening draws in.

festive supper

A light meal can be turned into a festive occasion with a little effort and plenty of imagination.

There are many occasions – over Christmas, for example – where you want to share a light meal with a few friends, but also to capture the atmosphere of the season.

Silk is a great fabric for a tablecloth at this sort of occasion – it has a certain decadent quality to it, and a metre of basic raw silk shouldn't be too expensive. As it frays easily, try pulling the loose threads to create a relaxed fringed edge on the sides that don't have the selvage. Make napkins to match from any left-over fabric and, if you want to make the table linen more decorative, sew on crystal or pearl beads in a loosely scattered pattern. Sequins will work just as well, too.

Roses look great on a festive supper table. Try placing a rose at each setting – either integrated with the napkin or standing in a dainty glass. And add to this some interesting table gifts, such as beaded pens or tiny decorative candles wrapped in tissue paper. Float small candles in dainty cut glassware and choose some pretty namecard holders.

left Choose unusual decorative objects as gifts for your guests, such as fragile glass baubles in each water glass, Perspex or glass droplets at each setting, and little mother-of-pearl boxes tied with ribbon.

this page, main This table has an almost magical quality, with the soft candlelight and pieces of dainty glassware and china. A tall dinner candle sits on an elegant drip tray with hanging droplets, and smaller candles sit in gilt wire holders and float in star cut-glass beakers in a ring above the settings.
below Sparkling glassware across the table will enhance the festive air of the occasion.
bottom Place large candles in storm lanterns or stemmed glass bowls and surround the base with rose petals or full rose heads.

exotic christmas spread

Red, green and gold are the traditional colours of Christmas. Employ them in unusual ways to create an exotic festive table.

Christmas is a special occasion for everyone. Though there are many possible themes for a table setting on this special day, a rich, sumptuous display will be enjoyed by all. Draw your colour inspirations from the traditional decorations of red berries, green holly and ivy and lots of gold, but adapt these themes using unusual objects and textures to make your setting a little bit different.

Try using a piece of gold organza as a table runner or buying banana leaves from an oriental supermarket and using these as a base for the setting. Exotic

opposite Reds, greens and golds look gorgeous laid out on this huge banana leaf. Hanging baubles and glass tealight holders carry the colour scheme higher.

left An abundance of candles, gold-wrapped chocolate coins and fruit – both artificial and fresh – make this a really festive setting.

below You don't have to have a Christmas tree – just decorate any suitable house plants.

As long as your elements fit into your chosen colour scheme of red, green and gold, you can't go wrong.

below Large wooden platters make great lay plates on this festive table and mark out each place setting. They are topped with an organza napkin, gift bag, bowl, cutlery and festive baubles.

right A centrally positioned light fitting is a good place from which to hang baubles on metallic ribbon and cord.

Twist flexible ivy around mirrors and picture frames and scatter individual holly leaves along a hearth or window ledge.

flowers are good at Christmas time as well. They are usually hardier and more durable than standard 'Christmas' flowers and there are many different festive shades to choose from. A single exotic stem will cost less than a traditional Christmas bouquet and will probably last longer. Collect holly and ivy from the garden or nearby woods and trail this around the area to be decorated. This greenery can also be tied around cutlery at each setting or circled around the base of a centrepiece.

Candles intensify the warmth and festivity of the occasion – at any time of the day or night. Choose warm colours and sit pillar candles on thick gold candlesticks and saucers. If you have any odd saucers or candleholders, why not invest in a can of gold spray paint and give everything a quick squirt to get into the festive spirit?

Table gifts are of utmost importance here. Make little gift bags from metallic organza and wrap tiny gifts to place as a surprise on each plate. Fortune cookies or foil-wrapped sweets will look enticing. Be creative when hanging your decorations, too. A tree is an obvious choice, but light fittings and picture rails are also good hanging places for Christmas decorations. And remember: even these don't have to be traditional – you could hang chocolates and fortune cookies for an unexpected twist. Just make sure your guests don't walk off with all your decorations!

below Pop a miniature bauble in the wineglass at each setting and use old wineglasses to hold small candles, propped up with a mixture of glitter and decorative red sand.
right Each set of cutlery has been tied together with gold string attached to a Christmas bauble.

far left If you run out of suitable holders, simply sit your candles in little pots of glitter for a festive display.
left These chocolates sit on a bed of crumpled clear cellophane for a magical touch.

new year's eve bash

New Year's Eve always calls for a party and is a good chance to exploit any themes that weren't used at Christmas.

Silver is always a good colour for New Year's Eve – particularly if you were enjoying an abundance of gold at Christmas. Choose another colour to go with the silver – pink or blue will work well – and aim to stick to these two colours.

Play around with different materials on the table top. Be funky with metal pie cases and foil take-away containers – easily found in household or freezer food shops. These will give the party less of a formal 'sit-down' feel, as guests pop outside to watch a firework display or leap up to play party games. Disposable napkins work well for this type of occasion, too. Make lay plates or mats for each setting by covering basic cork squares with tin foil or using inexpensive ready-foiled cake bases. Iridescent glitter, clear cellophane and lots of silver wrapping paper can be used to decorate the table top and surrounding surfaces.

Choose flowers that sit within your chosen colour scheme. You can buy dyed carnations or can spray white carnations with silver paint for a space-age effect, and float flower heads in a bowl with glowing gel candles.

left Layers of silver have been placed at each setting built up from a central runner made from metallic gift-wrapping paper.
above Here the colours of bright blue and silver have been rigidly adhered to to create a space-age setting. Even the sideboard has been covered in silver gift wrap to unite the whole scene.

right An elegant cocktail shaker is a practical and decorative necessity for this occasion. Glasses and tumblers are all decorated with fun metallic party pieces, such as streamers and miniature glitter balls. A bead curtain makes a great backdrop.

below A fun row of blue cocktails has been decorated with a skewered piece of banana leaf topped with kiwi fruit and an olive. Keep plenty of extra cocktails to hand in glass decanters to spread colour and ensure top-ups aren't far away.

cocktails and canapés

A stylish cocktail party is fun to plan for a birthday, Christmas or New Year's Eve celebration, or is a good way to liven up an ordinary Saturday night!

Plan a big buffet spread and theme everything from cutlery to ready-prepared drinks. Here it really is the presentation that counts.

Prepare little trays of snacks presented with candles and piles of pebbles. Look out for decorations tagged onto strands of pliable wire – these are great to wrap around knives and forks. Invest in a few banana leaves and cut these up to use as mats. Try layering elements, such as leaves, gravel and candles on plates and small dishes, so that each display is like a miniature 'garden'. Use anything flat and tray-like to offer drinks and snacks – coasters and shallow plates are ideal.

Candles in every shape and size are a must. Expand your colour palette to include blues, greens and reds so that everything is festive and bright. Invest in brightly coloured liqueurs and mixers and you can use these as your inspiration. Shake up a few cocktails, and the party will be well under way!

above left This spread has been laid out on a circular table to enable access from all angles. Everything has been placed in multiples to give lots of choice and plenty to see. The candles will be kept alight all through the evening, and a row of coloured fairy lights adds interest to the far wall.

above A selection of pineapple cubes is offered from a colourful tray. Each food offering has been decorated with candles, pebbles and leaves – all relatively inexpensive and very effective.

the settings

Modern mealtimes tend to be rather informal, but there are occasions when a more formal setting is appropriate. A table laid with row upon row of eating implements can seem daunting, but this need not be the case. Provided the table is laid correctly and you follow the simple rule of using the outermost utensil or utensils first, you can't go wrong. For this reason, a thoughtful host will lay the table carefully for a formal meal, so that no guest need feel embarrassed by making a mistake.

international informal

The most common setting for an informal Western meal positions the dinner knife to the right of the dinner plate with the soup spoon to the right of the knife. The dinner fork goes to the left of the plate, with the napkin neatly folded to the left of the fork. The pudding fork and spoon are then laid horizontally above the plate, the fork first with the handle to the left, and the spoon above it with the handle to the right.

1 Napkin in a simple fold
2 Dinner fork
3 Dinner plate
4 Dinner knife
5 Soup spoon
6 Pudding fork
7 Pudding spoon
8 White-wineglass
9 Red-wineglass
10 Water glass

British formal

A formal meal provides an opportunity to use lots of china and cutlery. If you have a large dining table, make full use of the space by laying the pudding spoon and fork inside the dinner knife and fork, and by including a butter plate to the left of the setting. The dinner knife and fork are used together in the European style, with the fork held in the left hand, tines down, and the knife held in the right hand for cutting and for guiding food onto the fork.

1 Napkin in a simple fold	7 Dinner knife
2 Butter plate	8 Soup spoon
3 Dinner fork	9 White-wineglass
4 Pudding fork	10 Red-wineglass
5 Dinner plate	11 Water glass
6 Pudding spoon	

English afternoon tea

For afternoon tea, the butter plate is placed centrally, with the napkin to the left, and the bread knife, pudding spoon and pastry fork – in that order – to the right-hand side of the plate. The teacup and saucer are set above the cutlery, with the teaspoon lying horizontally on the saucer behind the cup. The teacup handle should be sitting parallel to the teaspoon.

1 Napkin in a simple fold
2 Butter plate
3 Bread knife
4 Pudding spoon
5 Pastry fork
6 Saucer
7 Teacup
8 Teaspoon

American formal

This formal setting is for a three-course meal with a fish starter. A bread knife is optional, and would be laid on the butter plate. When eating the main course, the dinner fork is transferred to the right hand for each bite, and back to the left hand when the knife is required for cutting. Pudding utensils can also be laid across the top of the setting or brought in when pudding is served. It is not necessary to use both spoon and fork, but it may be easier.

1 Napkin in a simple fold	7 Dinner knife
2 Fish fork	8 Fish knife
3 Dinner fork	9 White-wineglass
4 Pudding fork	10 Red-wineglass
5 Dinner plate	11 Water glass
6 Pudding spoon	12 Butter plate

French formal

French settings differ from American and British in a number of ways. Butter plates and knives are not used, as bread is laid directly onto the table and butter is not served. Forks and spoons rest face down and a tablespoon is used in favour of the more familiar, rounded soup spoon. A knife rest is required so that the dinner knife can be laid back on the table, ready to be used for the cheese course, before pudding is served.

1 Napkin in a simple fold
2 Dinner fork
3 Pudding fork
4 Dinner plate
5 Pudding spoon
6 Dinner knife

7 Soup spoon
8 White-wineglass
9 Red-wineglass
10 Water glass

Chinese informal

For a Chinese meal, the chopsticks should be laid together to the right of the dinner plate, with the ends resting on a stand. The soup bowl and teacup are laid behind the plate, and a small dish for sauce is placed in front of the teacup. The soup spoon may be positioned in the bowl or at the side, to the left of the chopsticks. It is polite to offer guests who may be inexperienced with chopsticks the option of a knife and fork.

1 Dinner plate   5 Teacup
2 Chopsticks   6 Soup bowl
3 Chopstick stand   7 Soup spoon
4 Sauce dish   8 Saucer

Japanese informal

There are many possible settings for a Japanese meal, depending on the occasion and the food being served. For a basic setting, the rice bowl is on the left and the lidded soup bowl on the right. Fried or grilled foods are served in an open plate behind the rice bowl, with a small dish for pickle at the side. A cup for tea sits at the back on the right. Chopsticks lie horizontally resting side by side on a stand at the front, pointing to the left.

1 Rice bowl
2 Chopsticks
3 Chopstick stand
4 Soup bowl
5 Pickle dish
6 Teacup
7 Dinner plate

Suppliers

AFTER NOAH
121 Upper Street
London
N1 1QP
020 7359 4281
www.afternoah.co.uk
mailorder@afternoah.com
An eclectic mix of vintage and contemporary furniture and homeware

ALESSI
www.alessi.com
Italian designer homeware

BILL AMBERG
10 Chepstow Road
London
W2 5BD
020 7727 3560
Leather bags, luggage and products for the home

LAURA ASHLEY
256–258 Regent Street
London
W1R 5DA
0871 9835 999 for branches
0800 868 100 for mail order
www.lauraashley.com
A wide range of fashion, furnishings, fabrics and accessories for the home, alongside a complete interior design service

BENNISON FABRICS
16 Holbein Place
London
SW1W 8NL
020 7730 8076
Collection of late 17th- and 18th-century prints on linens and silks in muted colours, plus a small range of exclusive furniture

NINA CAMPBELL
9 Walton Street
London
SW3 2JD
020 7225 1105
f. 020 7225 0644
www.ninacampbell.com
Beautiful decorative accessories and furnishings for the home

CHRISTOFLE
10 Hanover Street
London
W1R 9HF
020 7491 4004
www.christofle.co.uk
Designer and producer of high-quality French porcelain, silverware, cutlery, table linen and crystal

THE CONRAN SHOP
Michelin House
81 Fulham Road
London
SW3 6RD
020 7589 7401
www.conranshop.co.uk
Design-led furniture, furnishings and accessories for the home and garden

DECORATIVE FABRICS GALLERY
278–280 Brompton Road
London
SW3 2AS
020 7589 4778
www.decorativefabrics.co.uk
www.monkwell.com
www.gp&jbaker.co.uk
Showroom for Monkwell and G P & J Baker fabrics and furnishings, alongside a good range of quality accessories for the home

DESIGNERS GUILD
261–271 & 275–277 King's Road
London
SW3 5EN
020 7351 5775
0845 6021189 for mail order
www.designersguild.com
An influential and creative force in the world of interior design with a unique approach to modern living

FITZROYS
77 Regent's Park Road
London
NW1 8UY
020 7722 1066
A beautiful, carefully chosen selection of flowers and antiques on sale; also offers an exclusive interior design service

THE FLOKATI RUG COMPANY
Unit 12, The Osiers Estate
Enterprise Way
Wandsworth
London
SW18 1EFJ
020 8337 3005
www.flokatirugco.co.uk
Specialists in 100 per cent pure wool pile woven flokati rugs

ANNA FRENCH
343 King's Road
London
SW3 5ES
020 7351 1126
www.annafrench.co.uk
A large range of fabrics and wallpapers with complementary furniture and accessories for the home

THE GENERAL TRADING COMPANY
2 Symons Street
London
SW3 2TJ
020 7730 0411
www.generaltradingcompany.co.uk
A large, interesting and diverse collection of quality goods for fashion and home, sourced from all over the world

HABITAT
196 Tottenham Court Road
London
W1P 9LD
0845 6010740 for branches
www.habitat.net
Stylish, inexpensive furnishings and accessories

HEAL'S
196 Tottenham Court Road
London
W1P 9LD
020 7636 1666 for branches
Contemporary furnishings and accessories

IMMACULATE HOUSE
Old Spitalfields Market
57/59 Brushfield Street
London
E1 6AA
020 7375 1844
Indulgent and decadent products for the home

CLEMENT JOSCELYNE
Market Square
Bishop's Stortford
CM23 3XA
01279 713000
www.clementjoscelyne.co.uk
Furniture Retailer of the Year in 1999 – offers a full interior design service alongside a fabulous range of home accessories and furniture

LIBERTY
214–220 Regent Street
London
W1R 6AH
020 7734 1234
www.liberty-of-london.com
An eclectic mix of products for the home, including a wide range of fabrics and trimmings

LOMBOK
555 King's Road
London
SW6 2EB
020 7736 0001
www.lombok.co.uk
Fantastic collection of affordable reclaimed teak furniture alongside original Javanese accessories

MacCULLOCH & WALLIS
25–26 Dering Street
London
W1R 0BH
020 7629 0311
www.macculloch-wallis.co.uk
Millinery, needlecraft and fabric specialists

MALABAR
(showroom address)
Unit 31–33
The Southbank Business Centre
Ponton Road
London
SW8 5BL
020 7501 4200 for stockists
info@malabar.co.uk
www.malabar.co.uk
Fantastic fabric range including wonderful hand-loomed cottons and sumptuous silks

DAVID MELLOR
4 Sloane Square
London
SW1W 8EE
020 7730 4259
www.davidmellordesign.co.uk
Specialists in award-winning cutlery, fine kitchenware and British crafts

MONSOON HOME
48 Brompton Road
London
SW3 1DP
020 7531 1408
www.monsoon.co.uk
Inspirational decorative pieces to adorn the home

MUJI
6–17 Tottenham Court Road
London
W1P 9DP
020 7436 1779
www.muji.co.uk
Practical and stylish household and fashion items from Japan

NORDIC STYLE
109 Lots Road
London
SW10 0RN
020 7351 1755
The widest selection of classic Swedish furniture, fabrics, wallpaper, paint, flooring and home accessories in the UK

OKA
The Coachworks
80 Parsons Green Lane
London
SW6 4HU
020 7348 7090
0870 160 6002 for mail order
www.okadirect.com
Simple and affordable furniture and accessories for the home

OPIUM
414 King's Road
London
SW10 0LJ
020 7795 0700
www.opiumshop.co.uk
A den of antique furniture and treasures from India and Southeast Asia

CHARLES PAGE
61 Fairfax Road
London
NW6 4EE
020 7328 9851
www.charlespage.co.uk
One of Europe's leading furniture stores, renowned for outstanding service, including a full interior design service

PAPERCHASE
213 Tottenham Court Road
London
W1P 9AF
020 7580 8496
0161 839 1500 for mail order
All types of paper, pens and card, plus namecards in a choice of colours

THE PIER
200 Tottenham Court Road
London
W1T 7PL
020 7637 7001
A good selection of affordable furniture and decorative accessories from around the world

POOLEY
29 Churton Street
London
SW1V 2LY
020 7828 3110
pooley-london.co.uk
A beautiful range of handmade hand-designed gifts for the home and yourself

PRICES
020 7228 3345 for stockists
Established in 1830, Price's Patent Candle Company is the UK's leading candle manufacturer and distributor

PURVES & PURVES
80–81 & 83 Tottenham Court Road
London
W1P 9HD
020 7580 8223 for mail order
www.purves.co.uk
Dinnerware, furniture and accessories

EMILY READETT-BAYLEY
01400 281563 for stockists
www.erbuk.com
A British designer working with Asian craftspeople and sustainable materials to produce an eclectic mix of homeware

ROBERTS
01709 571722 for stockists
www.robertsradio.co.uk
Radios combining traditional materials and skills with cutting-edge technology

HELENA ROHNER
c/Almendro 4
Madrid 28005
Spain
00 34 91365 7906
Handcrafted tableware in ceramic and wood

V.V. ROULEAUX
54 Sloane Square
Cliveden Place
London
SW1W 8AX
020 7730 3125
The ultimate shops for ribbons. Call for details of their other branches

SIA
0870 608 6060 for stockists
www.sia-deco.com
Home furnishings and accessories

TYPHOON
020 8974 4750 for stockists
www.typhooneurope.com
Wide range of alternative and oriental cookware, kitchen accessories and ceramics

VIADUCT
1–10 Summers Street
London
EC1R 5BD
020 7278 8456
www.viaduct.co.uk
Contemporary European furniture, accessories and lighting

VOODOO BLUE
Unit 10
Brentford Business Centre
Commerce Road
Brentford
TW8 8LG
020 8560 7050
www.voodooblue.co.uk
Design-led and carefully sourced fair-traded handwoven sisal and soapstone products from Kenya

WATERFORD CRYSTAL
Waterford Wedgwood
158 Regent Street
London
W1R 5SW
020 7734 7262
www.waterford.co.uk
Producers of fine-quality glassware, including collections designed by John Rocha

THE WEDDING LIST
91 Walton Street
London
SW3 2HP
0870 777 7000
www.theweddinglist.com
The Wedding List offers a fun and contemporary take on wedding lists and general gift-giving

JOANNA WOOD
48a Pimlico Road
London
SW1W 8LP
020 7730 5064
www.joannawood.com
Renowned interior designer with home-accessory shop

ARCHITECTS AND DESIGNERS WHOSE WORK IS FEATURED IN THIS BOOK

CUNNINGHAM FURNITURE
43 Davisville Road
London
W12 9SH
t./f. 020 8743 1972
m. 07957 468790
Pages: 52–54

ELIZABETH BLANK
Floral & Interior Designer
77 Regent's Park Road
London
NW1 8UY
020 7722 1066
Pages: 96–99

TAG ARCHITECTS
14 Belsize Crescent
London
NW3 5QU
020 7431 7974
Pages: 122–125

ROBERT DYE ASSOCIATES
Design Consultants/Chartered Architects
39–51 Highgate Road
London
NW5 1RS
020 7267 9388
f. 020 7267 9345
info@robertdye.com
www.robertdye.com
Pages: 104–107

MOOARC
198 Blackstock Road
London
N5 1EN
020 7354 1729
www.mooarc.com
Pages: 5, 50–51, 58–61

LEVITT BERNSTEIN ARCHITECTS
1 Kingsland Passage
London
E8 2BB
020 7275 7676
f. 020 7275 9348
www.levittbernstein.co.uk
Pages: 7, 70–73

Picture credits

5 the Rowlands family's house in London designed by MOOArc; 7 Aggie Mackenzie's kitchen in north London designed by Matthew Goulcher & Levitt Bernstein, built by LAD Construction; 8–9 Marian Cotterill's house in London; 50–51 the Rowlands family's house in London designed by MOOArc; 52–55 kitchen designed and supplied by Cunningham Furniture; 56–57 Sophy Hoare's house in London; 58–61 the Rowlands family's house in London designed by MOOArc; 66–69 Clare Mannix-Andrews's house in Hove; 70–73 Aggie Mackenzie's kitchen in north London designed by Matthew Goulcher & Levitt Bernstein, built by LAD Construction; 74–75 Clare Mannix-Andrews's house in Hove; 76–79 Ros Fairman's house in London; 82–85 Marian Cotterill's house in London; 92–95 Stephan Schulte's apartment at York Central in London; 96–99 an apartment in London designed by Elizabeth Blank; 100–103 Marian Cotterill's house in London; 104–107 Robert and Lucinda Dye's house in London designed by Robert Dye Associates; 112–115 Marian Cotterill's house in London; 116–119 Sophy Hoare's house in London; 120–121 Ros Fairman's house in London; 122–125 house in Hampstead designed by TAG Architects; 128–129 Stephan Schulte's apartment at York Central in London.

Index

Figures in *italics* refer to captions.

acknowledgements

First and foremost I would like to say thank you to David Brittain for his incredible and unfailing visual talent, support and friendship. Thanks also to Mark Kirk, who kept us laughing, and to Catherine Randy for lots of things, including her fantastic design skills and dedication.

Thanks to Debi Treloar and Louise Leffler for introducing me to Ryland Peters & Small, and to Gabriella Le Grazie for giving me such an enjoyable and inspiring opportunity. Finally, thanks to Sophie Bevan for her wonderful way with words.